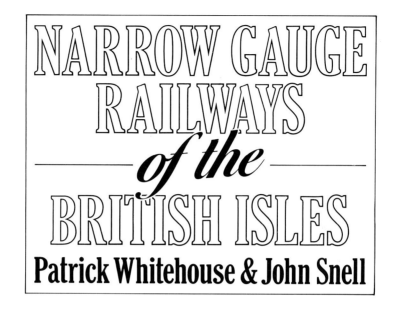

# NARROW GAUGE RAILWAYS *of the* BRITISH ISLES

## Patrick Whitehouse & John Snell

# NARROW GAUGE RAILWAYS *of the* BRITISH ISLES

## Patrick Whitehouse & John Snell

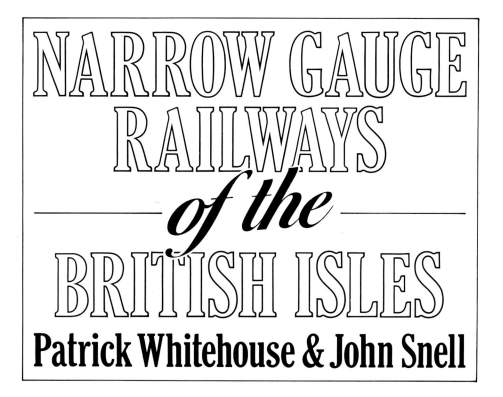

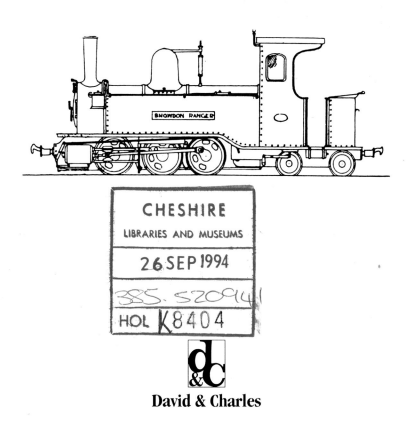

d&C
David & Charles

To James I.C. Boyd without whom we would be so much the poorer in narrow gauge history and lore.

This second edition is additionally dedicated to the memory of Patrick Whitehouse, another tireless railway historian and preservationist, who died just as work was starting on the revisions to the original text.

A David & Charles Book

Copyright © Millbrook House Ltd 1984, 1994

First published 1984
Second edition 1994

P.B. Whitehouse and J.B. Snell have asserted their right to be identified as authors of this work in accordance with the Copyright, Designs and Patents Act 1988.

A catalogue record for this book is available from the British Library.

ISBN 9 7153 0196 9

Typeset by XL Publishing Services, Nairn and printed in England by Butler & Tanner Ltd, Frome
For David & Charles
Brunel House Newton Abbot Devon

Frontispiece:
*Modern Day Festiniog Railway. Double-Fairlie locomotive built 1992* David Lloyd George *rounds the curve at Glan-y-Pwll with an afternoon train from Porthmadog to Blaenau Festiniog. Whilst the slate tips remain, the valley floor reflects little of the past.* P.J. Howard

# CONTENTS

# ACKNOWLEDGEMENTS

While a book of this nature endeavours to provide a differing slant on history it cannot change it. This book, for the first time, sets down the story of all the public narrow gauge railways of our Islands in partly evocative and partly historical form, up to but not including the modern 'preservation' era. Its aim is to get under the surface of the subject in a way that even photographs cannot, though these in themselves tell a pictorial story of some moment.

Inevitably there are links here with *Narrow Gauge Album* and *On the Narrow Gauge* because these pieces of evocative writing have been asked for as repeat works again and again. Experiences cannot be relived but they can be remembered and cherished. Thus some of the stories appearing in this book have seen print before, but two or three decades ago, so that a new generation will see them here for the first time. Our particular thanks here go out to John Powell (a co-author of the history of the Tralee & Dingle Railway) and Harold Vickers. Ted Patterson, too, has been a source of fascinating information as has that bard of the narrow gauge, James Boyd. Some extracts from articles previously published in the *Stephenson Locomotive Society Journal* have been used here and we would like to thank the then editor of this worthy magazine, Arthur Camwell, for permission to reproduce them. The same thing goes for the Irish Railway Record Society and R.N. Clements, without either of whom research in their fields would have been almost impossible. Other extracts are drawn from the magazine *Trains and Railways* and New English Library is thanked for permission to use these. Not all the pictures are new and this is by deliberate design — many are unique — either taken in an age where such photography was a rarity or for the story they tell. Other sources of information are provided in the bibliography and both authors are most grateful to the authors and publishers concerned. John Edgington and John Ransom have checked through the text to our heartfelt relief and gratitude. The line drawings by R.E. Tustin are available by courtesy of J.I.C. Boyd.

Finally we would like to thank the management and staff of all those lines we visited and enjoyed so long ago. We hope that this book will appeal not only to others with the same memories, but also to those who now enjoy, or work on, the remaining lines in their present form.

# PREFACE

In these Islands the narrow gauge railway, as envisaged by its progenitors, is now long dead: like most things devised by man, its usefulness was only temporary. Today we live in an age when few schoolboys want to be engine drivers and the romance of the railway has disappeared into a sponge of technology railways, except for those which carry vast numbers of commuters or fast impersonal InterCity expresses, are described as uneconomic in the passenger field: certainly in an age of the motor vehicle with its excellent roads paid for by the state the public and most businesses do not want to use other kinds of rail transport.

In spite of this, maybe because of it, there has been an upsurge of interest in railways as a hobby and the narrow gauge lines have their own share of devotees. The narrow gauge railway was cradled in the mountains of North Wales and its success and survival was due to one thing only – it was in those days economic. Most narrow gauge lines ran through poor and undeveloped countryside, were impecunious in the extreme and, above all, because they were often isolated they were individualistic and became the subjects of folklore. All these factors have built about the narrow gauge a fascination of its own and it was this which led a very small group of people including the authors of this book to be among the few who were in at the start of the modern revival on the Talyllyn Railway in 1951 .

Since then railway preservation and its venture into tourism has increased beyond the wildest dreams of those who pioneered the first lines. The man in the street has become narrow gauge conscious – his holiday trips to North Wales, the Isle of Man and the Lake District have seen to that; while even more has been achieved in standard gauge railway preservation. The success of the pioneer tourist lines has encouraged some to imitate, has dismayed others (who found that the past could not be recreated in every detail) and has surprised everyone. The biggest shock was the discovery that they really *were* in the railway business and that owning and running a railway is a heavy and relentless responsibility which cannot be declined, for the trains must be kept running. Nothing could run (or did run) without spending money; this meant income was needed. To obtain this from the public it is vital to provide a reliable train service, comfortable stock and safe working practices. There can be no half measures in this field. Either a railway captures the traffic it wants (or wanted) or it fails; once there was basically freight, now tourists make the payload. Gone are the 'good old days' (in any case they were infrequently good) and in their place today is a new challenge laced with some pleasure and excitement.

But has this new business succeeded? The answer must be, yes, though as of old the narrow gauge railway of today maintains an uneasy financial equilibrium and must exist on less capital funds and equipment than it would like. On the other side of the scales there is an almost unbelievable determination in the new managements (many of whom are volunteers) to press forward and to succeed. Both authors of this book once asked the question – 'will the next generation come forward with the necessary enthusiasm and love of hard work when their turn comes to take over?' Fortunately once again the answer has been a resounding yes. Even so those who are interested in keeping these historic railways going will have to continue (as did their fathers, grandfathers and great grandfathers) to look at investment into the future, and even if that future lies in the hands of youth, they too will have to be business-like.

This book has been written to attempt to set out in one volume something both of the ambience and the history of our narrow gauge railways up to the time, a single generation ago, when that new spirit was born. By covering the whole of the British field it cannot go into deep detail on any individual line, but there are many erudite works which can, and do, specialise in particular railways and areas. But if this book rekindles or starts an interest in its subject our labours will have been more than worthwhile.

PBW/JBS

*The survival of the narrow-gauge lines has mainly been due to the vastly increased tourist market during the last thirty years. Now rebuilt to 12¼in gauge the Fairbourne and Barmouth Steam Railway presents a new image at Porth Penrhyn. The Barmouth Ferry leaves from the nearby beach for the short journey across the Afon Mawddach. The 0–4–0ST* Sherpa *was built by Milner Engineering in 1978. A 2–6–2T based on the Lynton and Barnstaple locomotive* Yeo *also operates on the new line.*
P.J. Howard

# PROLOGUE

You cannot get to Portmadoc without passing through some of the best scenery in Wales. By whichever route you arrive, Beddgelert and the Welsh Highland way, over the Crimea Pass or the high Bala road and through Blaenau or on the coastal railway through Harlech, the country can scarcely fail to impress.

For those with an ear to history it is also an exciting place; yet how many remember that the other approach, the most used during the town's great days, is now no longer used? Once the ships came in past Borth-y-Gest and the Ballast Bank and men made the harbour to protect them from the sea. To bring cargo to those ships they built the Festiniog Railway so that slate from the mountains of Blaenau could roof towns and villages throughout these islands. Few of these holidaymakers visiting the town now care one jot that the railway serving Maddocks' port once influenced communications throughout the world. Yet this is true and it is salutary to reflect that those two rails two feet apart which run the length of the Cob, straight as a die, helped to spread the industrial revolution and bring a brief measure of prosperity to this remote part of the Principality.

Nostalgia is a disease which increases with the passing years, often coupled with an enthusiasm for rusting rails and derelict road-beds leading to visions of a state of economic bliss which never was; but with the new Festiniog almost 40 years established one must resist the tendency to hark hack to the good old days. For one thing, after about 1910 the old company had few good days and in some ways it is the present which constitutes the railway's zenith. Yet somehow it is difficult to keep down a feeling of regret that the long slate sheds adjoining the harbour are no longer there and that the station yard is hemmed in with modern concrete holiday homes. If only one could wish hard enough to see just one more loaded gravity train trundle inexorably round that spectacularly banked curve at Boston Lodge – but no, that is gone forever. The trains still run now for one reason only – that a sufficient number of customers want them to, aided and abetted of course by the vital volunteers and the Wales Tourist Board.

During the summer of 1934 young Pat Whitehouse, having done a little research and in the belief that the Festiniog was to the mountains of Wales what the 4ft 8½in gauge was to the rest of the country, talked his parents into allowing him to make his first solo train journey, part of it over the greatest white elephant of them all, the Welsh Highland Railway.

At this time posters on stations, including Birmingham New Street

*Festiniog Railway advertising between the wars. A poster by Norman Keene showing a trainload of cheerful passengers despite the horrifying drop on one side and the apparently unsecured track in front.*
Millbrook House collection

*Dinas Junction, in 1925, two years after the opening of the Welsh Highland Railway. On the left, with the new railway's name emblazoned on the side of freshly painted bogie coaches and the North Wales Narrow Gauge Railway 0–6–4 single Fairlie* Moel Tryfan *at its head, is the Welsh Highland train. On the right the Caernarvon to Afon Wen branch of the erstwhile LNWR – now LMS, with the standard train set – a Webb 18in goods and equally ancient non corridor coaches. The locomotive has not yet been repainted in its post grouping livery and carries an LNWR cast number plate on its cab side. The station nameboard, again pristine, reads as it would have done in the old days of the NWNGR – Dinas Junction change for Snowdon & Beddgelert – no mention is made of the further delights including the Aberglaslyn Pass and Portmadoc.*
C.J. Keylock collection

**FESTINIOG RAILWAY**

and the North Wales resorts, were advertising 'a trip through Faery Land', using the metals of the LMS to Bangor and Dinas Junction, where changes of train were made for Portmadoc (Porthmadog in the Welsh spelling) and Blaenau Ffestiniog, with the homeward journey via the Conway Valley branch to Llandudno Junction. After much study of the timetable (for the Welsh Highland service in particular was very meagre) it was found that the 10.40am from Bangor could begin the adventure and the explorer set out on one of the most fascinating journeys of his life. The train of Victorian vintage blasted its throaty way up to Dinas Junction where passengers surged across the platform to pack the sagging coaches of the adjacent Welsh Highland train. In the distance lay a corrugated iron shed and from this derelict building the schoolboy's first narrow gauge 'cop', cylinder cocks open and yellow smoke oozing from her chimney, crept towards the train: it proved to be the North Wales Narrow Gauge Railway's 0–6–4T *Moel Tryfan*. With a clang and a jar she coupled to her coaches, raising shrieks of mock alarm from her indulgent passengers and, at 11.25am, the aged guard signalled the right away. *Moel Tryfan* slipping and hissing, climbed past the shed on the right, rounded the long curved cutting and set course for Waenfawr.

The rainbow painted coaches, with the guard climbing along the running boards, a rack of tickets his only uniform, and the grass grown track proclaimed no main line railway but rather one in mortal decline; so the schoolboy glued his eyes and ears to what mattered. A quick dash across the platform at Dinas Junction had secured him a corner seat granting ecstatic views of whirling rods as *Moel Tryfan* plodded on up the impressive climb past Quellyn Lake to South Snowdon. Here most passengers disembarked to investigate a commotion which had appeared at the rear end: a resistant knot was undone, a two stroke motor broke into life, the PW gang of semicentenarians climbed into position and chugged sideways down the hill so laboriously climbed by *Moel Tryfan*. The Col Stephens trolley disappeared round the bend to a derisive chorus from the gallery.

At Beddgelert there was a six minute wait while the fire was cleaned and here the schoolboy managed to talk the crew into allowing him a footplate ride for the remainder of the journey. Years later John Snell incautiously wrote (much to the fury of readers of the *Cambrian News*) that a special race of pygmies was bred to man Welsh narrow gauge engines; certainly young Patrick, comparatively tall, found his hair giving the cab such a cleaning as it never had for years. *Moel Tryfan* leaked steam from everywhere and outside it was raining hard so there was not much scenery to see, but the 0–6–4 tank's unpredictable acceleration after descending through the Aberglaslyn Pass and Nantmor Tunnel busily sped her train along the four straight and dull level miles into Portmadoc (New) station. There followed a long and dreary walk across the GWR and through the dripping wet town, in time to see the Festiniog's red painted dirty double engine *Merddin Emrys* appear out of the driving mist enveloping the Cob and back on to its train at the Harbour station.

There was just time enough to get a ticket before being locked into

11

*Welsh Highland Railway timetable for 1934. Note the sparsity of trains – three in each direction making connections with the LMS Bangor to Afon Wen line. This notice dated June 1934 states in small print at the bottom: 'the Welsh Highland Railway is operated by the Festiniog Railway.' Note also the Five Valley circular tour advertisement.*
Millbrook House collection

Bottom right:
*Welsh Highland Railway 1935. A train near the south end of the Aberglaslyn pass with platelayers' trolley attached to the rear.*
H.F. Wheeller

Bottom left:
*Welsh Highland Railway train staff ticket in use when the section to Portmadoc (Porthmadog) Harbour station was in operation. On the back is a notice: 'This ticket must be given up by the Engine Driver or Brakesman immediately on arrival to the person in charge of the Station to which he is authorised to proceed and at the end of the day the Tickets must be sent to the Traffic Office Portmadoc. H.F. Stephens, Managing Director.'*
Millbrook House collection

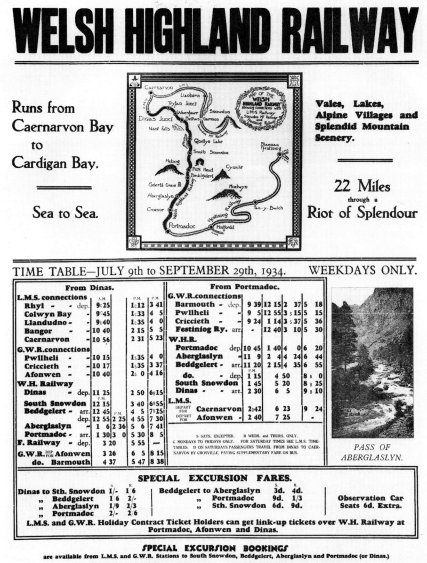

# WELSH HIGHLAND RAILWAY

**Runs from Caernarvon Bay to Cardigan Bay.**

**Sea to Sea.**

**Vales, Lakes, Alpine Villages and Splendid Mountain Scenery.**

**22 Miles** through a **Riot of Splendour**

### TIME TABLE—JULY 9th to SEPTEMBER 29th, 1934. WEEKDAYS ONLY.

**From Dinas.**

| L.M.S. connections | | A.M. | P.M. | P.M. |
|---|---|---|---|---|
| Rhyl - | dep. | 9.25 | 1.12 | 3 41 |
| Colwyn Bay | - | 9.45 | 1.33 | 4 5 |
| Llandudno | - | 9.40 | 1.35 | 4 0 |
| Bangor | - | 10 40 | 2 15 | 5 5 |
| Caernarvon | - | 10 56 | 2 31 | 5 23 |
| **G.W.R. connections** | | | | |
| Pwllheli | - | 10 15 | 1.35 | 4 0 |
| Criccieth | - | 10 17 | 1.35 | 3 37 |
| Afonwen | - | 10 40 | 2.0 | 4 16 |
| **W.H. Railway** | | | P.M. | |
| Dinas - | dep. | 11 25 | 2 50 | 6.15 |
| South Snowdon | arr. | 12 15 | 3 40 | 6.55 |
| Beddgelert - | arr. | 12 45 | 4 5 | 7.25 |
| | dep. | 12 55 | 2 25 | 4 55 | 7 30 |
| Aberglaslyn | - | 1 6 | 2 36 | 5 6 | 7 41 |
| Portmadoc - | arr. | 1 30 | 3 0 | 5 30 | 8 5 |
| F. Railway - | dep. | 3 20 | | 5 55 | |
| G.W.R. DEP. FOR Afonwen | | 3 26 | | 6 5 | 8 15 |
| do. Barmouth | | 4 37 | | 5 47 | 8 38 |

**From Portmadoc.**

| G.W.R. connections | | | | | | |
|---|---|---|---|---|---|---|
| Barmouth - | dep. | 9 39 | 12 15 | 2 37 | 5 18 |
| Pwllheli - | , | 9 5 | 12 55 | 3 s 15 | 5 15 |
| Criccieth - | , | 9 24 | 1 14 | 3 37 | 5 36 |
| Festiniog Ry. | arr. | - | 12 40 | 3 10 | 5 30 |
| **W.H.R.** | | | | | | |
| Portmadoc | dep. | 10 45 | 1 40 | 4 0 | 6 20 |
| Aberglaslyn | - | 11 9 | 2 4 | 4 24 | 6 44 |
| Beddgelert - | arr. | 11 20 | 2 15 | 4 35 | 6 55 |
| do. - | dep. | 1 15 | | 4 50 | 8 B 0 |
| South Snowdon | | 1 45 | | 5 20 | 8 B 25 |
| Dinas - | arr. | 2 30 | | 6 5 | 9 B 10 |
| **L.M.S.** | | | | | | |
| DEPART FOR Caernarvon | | 2.42 | | 6 23 | 9 24 |
| DEPART FOR Afonwen - | | 2 40 | | 7 25 | - |

S SATS. EXCEPTED. B WEDS. and THURS. ONLY.
C MONDAYS TO FRIDAYS ONLY. FOR SATURDAY TIMES SEE L.M.S. TIME-TABLES. D ON SATURDAYS PASSENGERS TRAVEL FROM DINAS TO CAERNARVON BY CROSVILLE, PAYING SUPPLEMENTARY FARE ON BUS.

*PASS OF ABERGLASLYN.*

### SPECIAL EXCURSION FARES.

| | S. | R. | | S. | R. | | |
|---|---|---|---|---|---|---|---|
| Dinas to Sth. Snowdon | 1/- | 1 6 | Beddgelert to Aberglaslyn | 3d. | 4d. | | |
| " Beddgelert | 1 6 | 2/- | " Portmadoc | 9d. | 1/3 | Observation Car | |
| " Aberglaslyn | 1/9 | 2/3 | " Sth. Snowdon | 6d. | 9d. | Seats 6d. Extra. | |
| " Portmadoc | 2/- | 2/6 | | | | | |

L.M.S. and G.W.R. Holiday Contract Ticket Holders can get link-up tickets over W.H. Railway at Portmadoc, Afonwen and Dinas.

### SPECIAL EXCURSION BOOKINGS

are available from L.M.S. and G.W.R. Stations to South Snowdon, Beddgelert, Aberglaslyn and Portmadoc (or Dinas.)

### SPECIAL TICKETS FOR FIVE VALLEY CIRCULAR TOUR

are issued from L.M.S. Stations via Dinas or Blaenau Festiniog, over Welsh Highland and Festiniog Railways embracing Conway, Lledr, Maentwrog, Glaslyn and Gwyrfai Valleys, also

CIRCULAR TOUR from G.W.R Stations via Portmadoc over Welsh Highland Railway to Dinas thence by L.M.S. to Afonwen, and to destination or vice-versa.

HIKERS TOUR TICKET also available to South Snowdon, whence to ascend Snowdon afoot, returning from Summit by Snowdon Mountain Railway to Llanberis.

For details of all Excursions and Tours see Bills at L.M.S. and G.W.R. Stations, or from Festiniog Railway, Portmadoc.

The Company give notice that they do not undertake that the trains will start or arrive at the times specified on the Time Tables, nor will they be accountable for any loss, inconvenience or injury which may arise from delays or detentions, but every endeavour will be made to ensure punctuality as far as practicable. Passengers booking at intermediate stations can only do so conditionally upon there being room in the train.

The Welsh Highland Railway is operated by Festiniog Railway.

PORTMADOC, June 1934.

R. EVANS, Traffic Manager.

**WELSH HIGHLAND RAILWAY.**

**TRAIN STAFF TICKET.**

**TRAIN No.** _____ **(DOWN)**

To the **Engine Driver** or **Brakesman**

You are authorised, after seeing the Train Staff colored **Blue** for the Section, to proceed from

**Portmadoc** (Old Station) to **Portmadoc** (New Station)

and the Train Staff will follow.

Signature of person in charge..........................

Date........................19

(over)

a third class compartment full of equally dripping adults. The journey to Blaenau Ffestiniog was enlivened at Minffordd by a party of campers who took possession of part of the train, following one another out of the windows of the locked doors, over the roof and back into the windows on the other side much to the fury of the guard who rightly feared for the consequences if this was attempted while the train was in motion. *Merddin Emrys* slipped violently and lost time all the way, the steam emerging from her joints combining with the mist effectively to blot out any sight of the Vale of Ffestiniog and making the passage of the narrow-bored Moelwyn Tunnel an experience not to be repeated voluntarily. This was always nasty; but in later days one learned to sit in the front coach – indeed the front compartment if possible – where the smoke was carried over and past, to listen with joyful anticipation for the shrieks from the rear vehicles when suffocation appeared imminent. The LMS men holding the Llandudno Junction connection at Blaenau were not amused and barely waited for the passengers to join it.

During the return trip on the standard gauge train a man in the compartment asked the schoolboy what he had been doing – and had he looked in the mirror recently. Very fortunately this was a corridor

*Driver's eye view. Double Fairlie No 3* Earl of Merioneth *emerges from Garnedd tunnel, Festiniog Railway.*
Festiniog Railway Company

coach so he did his best in the toilet with such soap and towels as were available but the arrival back at the hotel did not produce a great welcome – it took three days to get the soot and grease out of his hair and the hotel pillowcases suffered accordingly. But it was an introduction to a new world.

In the autumn of 1946, having been released from his King's Shilling, the erstwhile schoolboy headed for Wales once again only to find that things were black. In June a ship had actually called at Portmadoc, the first for years, but it was a nine day wonder never to be repeated. On 1 August the last Festiniog men were given notice as they put the ancient 0–4–0 saddle tank *Prince* back into the shed; the railway lay derelict and gloomy. The Welsh Highland had been taken up during the war and only earthworks remained: memory alone would see *Prince* and *Princess* in their extreme old age labouring up that frightful twisting climb, far steeper than anything they had ever faced before, to Pitts Head, struggling with three or four bogie coaches of holiday-makers. With the Festiniog gone the last survivor was the equally ancient and almost equally derelict Talyllyn further down the coast; but this still ran and its rediscovery and survival is another and often told story.

However, there was still a narrow gauge railway or two, even if across the sea in Ireland. A check back through the May issues of *The*

*A double Fairlie (probably No 10* Merddin Emrys *then painted red) emerging from Garnedd tunnel in the mid 1930s. The photograph clearly shows the good condition of the Festiniog Railway's track and fencing even in those impecunious days.* P.B. Whitehouse

*Not dead but sleeping. The old Festiniog Railway Boston Lodge shed on 3 August 1952 when the line lay derelict after closure in 1946. On the left is the Welsh Highland 0–6–4 tank* Moel Tryfan, *sadly broken up by the new management, and to the right double Fairlie 0–4–4–0 tank No 10* Merddin Emrys *later to be rebuilt and now in service as an oil burner.* E.S. Russell

*Railway Magazine* (the May issues at that time were usually devoted to Irish matters) showed some fascinating possibilities: the wild and little recorded Letterkenny & Burtonport Extension Railway in Donegal, the West Clare of music hall fame and, wonder of wonders, a full page frontispiece of a cattle special on the far western Tralee & Dingle Railway. To add to temptation was the publication of the first real enthusiast's book – Fayle's *Narrow Gauge Railways of Ireland.* No one knew it then but there was barely a decade to go.

A long weekend in 1949 began by train to Liverpool and night boat to Dublin, with next morning's bacon and eggs in a mahogany dining car on the Great Northern, the engine a sky blue and scarlet 4–4–0 bound for Belfast. Thence to Derry and a walk to the Victoria Bridge station of the 3ft gauge County Donegal Railways. It was a temporary glance into an old world.

The West Clare's daily mixed train for windswept Moyasta Junction and the coast left Ennis at 4.55pm if the connecting 5ft 3in gauge train from Limerick was on time, which happened often enough for the locals not to worry. The coaches, period pieces all, sat in the bay platform slowly filling with farmers with pipes, their womenfolk puffing at cigarettes and schoolchildren (some 80 of them) on their way home from their daily sojourn with the Holy Sisters. All the ex West Clare Railway vehicles were six wheelers, one a clerestory–roofed saloon, still in Great Southern maroon with that company's arms emblazoned on the doors, the brake van a transplanted Tralee & Dingle bogie vehicle in CIE green with the flying snail totem in yellow. The first class compartments were products of a bygone age, seats covered in black American cloth well studded with buttons, and braided arm rests looped on the door pillars, while the captions of the elderly photographs over the heads of the seats were handwritten in fading copperplate. Shortly before the broad gauge

and ancient McDonnel 4–4–0 rolled alongside the opposite platform face, an outside cylindered 4–6–0 tank built in 1922, but designed by W. J. Carter, Consulting Engineer to the West Clare in 1903 and now numbered 3C, crept down from the shed beyond the road bridge and coupled on to the gas lit coaches. The Tralee & Dingle van was more modern, having electric lights, though the dynamo was missing these many years past.

Looping west past the still active workshops the train plunged into a countryside calculated to break any farmer's heart. The coaches, apart from the first class seats, gave a ride which would be considered only adequate on the 2ft gauge Festiniog. First stop Corofin, to pass the homeward bound daily goods behind an earlier 0–6–2 tank No 5C, the train carefully blocked the level crossing, providing a pleasant diversion and causing no annoyance to the waiting two-wheeled donkey carts piled high with turf. Up over the stony hillside then curving down to Ennistymon for water and on to Lahinch with its station high above the beach. This was the line's one tourist stop, with a golden strand crooked in the elbow of Liscannor Bay. As 3C panted her way up the long climb from the sea a glance at the wild Irishmen joining the train at Ennistymon turned English thoughts towards the next stop at Milltown Malbay, the last station large enough to have two platforms, where passengers could look down on Spanish Point to contemplate the pitiless destruction, in 1588, of six proud Spanish galleons caught in the fury of the Atlantic gales: they were plundered without mercy. Down then to the coast at Quilty over almost treeless heathland to see black upturned curraghs lying on the beach. Here gales were so strong at times that a special anemometer was installed at the station, ringing a danger bell if wind velocity reached over 60mph when no train could run unless its coaches were specially weighed down with slabs of concrete; the knowledgeable passenger looked for special white diamonds on the coach frames before leaving Ennis. At 80mph a second bell would ring and all trains were stopped; once, in 1927, 93mph was recorded.

*Victoria Bridge Station, Londonderry with the CDRJC train made up of 2–6–4 tank No 2* Blanche *and two coaches standing alongside the island platform. This section to Strabane was technically owned by Ulster Transport Authority (UTA) at that time since it was wholly Midland in origin. The date of the photograph is Whitsun 1949.* P.B. Whitehouse

Spirits rose in the clear and heady air of the Atlantic seaboard with brown briquette smoke drifting from 3C's chimney as she hurried out along the boglands through Kilmurry, Cragganock and Doonbeg; here in this lonely windswept land the train became a magnet, the inhabitants rising from turf and stone like leprechauns of old; the great event of the day was 'to meet the train'.

It would be getting dark as the little train crossed the long narrow peninsula terminating in Loop Head to arrive almost unexpectedly into the triangle of railway lines – a sort of Island state consisting of a few houses with the inevitable bar – which was Moyasta Junction. Across the platform face stood the Kilrush train headed probably by one of the three 1898 2–6–2 tanks built by T. Green & Son Ltd of Leeds. You seemed to have two choices of weather – dripping gloom or the magnificence of hailstones penetrated by wonderful visions of sunshine shafts. In the season the holidaymakers made for Kilkee, for after all it had a strand. The crew of the 2–6–2T now headed towards

*West Clare 4–6–0 tank no 3C (once named* Ennistymon) *takes water adjacent to a dual purpose tank at Ennis station in the summer of 1952. This Hunslet engine was built in 1922 and was along with its sister No 7C (*Malbay*) the last built for any Irish narrow gauge railway. With 0–6–2 tanks Nos 5C and 6C* Slieve Callan *and* Saint Senan (*of Scattery Island Kilrush*) *they were the regular engines on the main line of the West Clare section during the later years of steam.*
P.B. Whitehouse

17

Kilrush, their single coach swinging behind them over the lonely saltings, skirting the harbour with its glimpse of the ruined monastery on Scattery Island. There was once an extension to Cappagh Pier whence, in Percy French's day, boats plied to Limerick and civilisation.

But if the West Clare was in the vernacular 'a grand railway' there was one further south which was even grander: it ran from Tralee westwards through the green Kerry mountains to the remote fishing village of Dingle. It was the last Irish 3ft gauge railway to have its main line running for a considerable part along the rough public road. When its harbour branch was open, it was the most westerly railway in Europe. Its engines needed the faculties of a Kerry goat, it was perpetually in the red, and it was a strong contender for the title which Percy French unjustly bestowed on the West Clare. By the time this delightful piece of Irishism had become known to the erstwhile schoolboy it was, for certain, the last piece of adventurous railroading to be found in these islands.

Early in 1939 men had come from the County Council to pave the Dingle road, and this coupled with the fact that if rail passenger services were to continue to run the permanent way would need to be relaid completely, made up the minds of those in charge of the Great Southern Railways. The nuisance could not be disposed of because of considerable fair day cattle traffic, but it could be mitigated. It was. By the end of the 'Emergency' (the second world war which did not involve what was then the Irish Free State) a daily goods was still running, but the 1947 fuel famine put a stop to that. Only the monthly trains serving the Dingle cattle fair remained. This was an occasion needing all the resources of the railway, men, machines and stock. Often they were not enough, especially during the latter part of the summer when traffic was heaviest. By then the sparse amount of grass on the stony peninsula was getting even sparser and the animals were sent to the lush green lands of the Midlands for fattening. Such quantities could only come out by rail. This meant that until the very last years four engines sat in Tralee shed and for the monthly summer specials all four had to be steamed, each train needing to be double

18

headed over the dreadful misty mountains, in parts on gradients steeper than 1 in 30. When engine shortages became acute on the West Clare they sent 6T north to Ennis after an overhaul at Inchicore and that left the foreman at Tralee mainline shed, to which the branch was attached, some nasty permutations to solve. It was at such a time that they lost a chimney.

This happened to 2T (they were all Hunslet 2–6–0 tanks by then and each engine carried the suffix T to denote the section) which had been left for a time with her chimney under a hole in the roof in Tralee narrow gauge shed; the occasion certainly dates from the time when they had enough serviceable wagons for the two double-headed specials or even two double-headed and another, but only three engines – whatever their condition. It was early autumn (and a vital time to get the cattle out) with had mists and damp grass making the rail slippery and life very difficult. The engine concerned got to Dingle on the Friday, completed the next day's shunt in the yard and coupled on to the head of the train engine for the journey back but on the climb up towards Anascaul they ran out of sand and stuck. This meant that the long suffering Garrett, the loco foreman at Tralee, had to go out to them with a lorry and more sand; this happened twice at least which makes one suspect two double-headed specials. Finally, 2T made her way back to Dingle, bunker first to save time, to help get the last train out. It was now dark and the Saturday Fair had been a

*Reproduced as a frontispiece in the May 1939 issue of* The Railway Magazine *this evocative photograph sparked off one of the author's imagination and a determination to see what was lying over the water. The picture taken on 29 April 1938 shows a cattle special on the erstwhile Tralee & Dingle section of what was then the Great Southern Railways of Ireland. The scene is near Camp at the foot of the infamous Glenagalt incline rising up from Castlegregory Junction at 1 in 31 and 1 in 30. The train headed by Hunslet 2–6–0 tanks Nos 1T and 2T is rounding a deviation curve constructed after a loaded cattle special had run away on 22 May 1893, coming to grief on an over-sharp curve seen here in the form of a derelict viaduct bridge below and to the left of the leading engine.*
W.A. Camwell

great one. Anyway it was quite late at night when Garrett's phone rang again – it was the stationmaster at Dingle.

'The engine has lost its chimney and the driver wants to know what to do?'

'Impossible. You must have got it wrong. Get me the driver.'

He was fetched.

'What the bloody hell's all this?'

'When I got back here the chimney was gone – what will I do?'

'Nothing I can do about it, come back home best you can'.

So they set out gingerly from Dingle with the train, one engine doing the hard work and smoke blowing all over the place and sure enough a couple of miles out there was the chimney lying between the rails. They picked it up and threw it on the front and strangely enough she steamed all right. But they ran out of sand again and were back in Tralee just in nice time for mass on Sunday morning!

Travel by road now from Tralee to Dingle and you have to look hard for the evidence that a railway ever ran there. The CIE bus, doing a good 50mph, will be in Dingle in an hour and a half whereas the train of the 1930s would have done it in $2\frac{1}{2}$. It is worth reflecting, just one more time, on the last days of the railway when the monthly cattle trains ran and its life hung in the balance by this single thread. The maximum load for the line was 18 vehicles made up of 17 cattle vans and one ex passenger brake converted into part cattle wagon, part guard's van. This was adapted by the erection of a crude waist high partition protecting the guard from too intimate an association with the livestock. At least one of the remaining vans had the handbrake screw smack in the middle of the cattle portion. On discovering this the language of any non Dingle man who got shanghaied on to the job had to be heard to be believed. Nevertheless as far as possible the section was worked by ex T & D crews and certainly by Great Southern men who were allocated to it in earlier years; normal broad gauge men could not be bribed into doing it. The only remaining true T & D driver was Billy Hanlon, who worked the trip regularly and whose home was still at Dingle, 31 miles from his place of work – a lodging turn in reverse. To ride on the footplate of one of the two engines was an experience scarcely believable, though long cherished and relished, while, once made, the journey ensured that any stranger would side with the broad gauge men in Tralee.

Billy Hanlon would usually have 8T, the pilot and 1T was the train engine with 2T held very much in reserve, even after her chimney had been re-attached. The first job was to oil round, paying particular attention to the coupled axleboxes which were tricky. The ritual was to insert a 'spout' of folded tin between the wheel spokes which acted as a channel to carry the oil on to the box crown. Meanwhile the fireman was making up the fire, evidence of which was only too apparent in the form of a trail of sulphurous yellow smoke smothering the cab and wandering lazily from the tall chimney. Both engines appeared unkempt, their black paint overlaid with grime. In due course each made its way through the station loop crossed over Ashe Street and ran along the road past Latchfords Mill to the interchange

yard for coal in front of the main station. Shovelling from a broad gauge wagon filled the tiny bunkers at the rear of the side tanks and covered the floor of the cabs to a depth of about 18in with lumps and slack, just allowing one door to open; briquettes were piled on top of the side tanks, firebox, and over the front platform under the smokebox door. Then back to the narrow gauge station, protected from unsuspecting motorists by the fireman walking in front with a red flag.

The Special Traffic notice said that the train would depart from Tralee at 11.00am but the regular visitor knew better: the men would not leave until after they had been paid. Surely enough after the hustle and bustle of the preparations everything went quiet, with scarcely a member of the staff to be seen. Then, around midday things came to life again, shovels clanged against fireholes, smoke became blacker and they were off over Rock Street Level crossing to make their semi-circular exit through the back of Tralee. The engines were taken under easy steam, nosing along at 15–20mph with the decrepit wagons bucketing along behind them. The footplate visitor watched the water bobbing up and down in the unprotected gauge glass

*A homeward bound cattle special on the 3ft 0in gauge Tralee & Dingle section of the CIE. These trains ran out on the last Friday of each summer month returning after Dingle Fair on the Saturday. This photograph is taken at Lispole Viaduct at the foot of the 1 in 29 climb up to Garrynadur. Officially, since 1929, this bridge was considered unsafe for double headed trains and the practice forbidden. However, not only had the horse its head towards the stable but tackling the gradient from a standing start was not a thought which entered locomotive crews' heads in June 1950. P.B. Whitehouse*

21

thinking of the indemnity form he had recently signed over a sixpenny stamp. The ejector could only maintain about 17in of vacuum – in the brake van with leakage on the way it was seldom more than 14in. But it seemed moderately effective.

Beyond the Basin on the left rose the mountains of the Slieve Mish, crowned by the 3127ft Mount Brandon. To the right lay Tralee Bay, azure in the summer sun. Slow at Blennerville platform, whistle and cross the gateless Dingle road (almost blind in one direction) through a dirt lane by the old windmill tower and sharply round to the left to the Dingle road again, only to cross it suddenly just before the bend at Tonevane crossroads, three miles out. The journey was now along-side the road in true tramway style, occasionally swinging in startling fashion from one side to the other (originally the engines had metal skirts over the motion to avoid frightening the livestock too much.) Motorists needed all their wits about them for there were no crossing gates and the trains in no way slackened speed. There were, of course, the usual scenes of alarm and excitement when horses and other straying livestock were encountered, some bent on suicide. The usual way of dealing with these was by shouts, loud whistles and wild gestures from both ends of the train, but if all else failed the fireman would climb up on the coal bunker lid and pelt the offenders with briquettes.

The mountains shimmered in the warm sun while on the right stretched Derrymore Strand, miles of beautiful golden sandy beach; the train hammered up the rise to Derrymore then ran more easily until the home signal for Castlegregory Junction came into sight. It snaked across the road at another unprotected crossing to stop in the loop 40 minutes out of Tralee. By the time the engines had clanked to a stop 8T's fireman would be out on the tank top ready to drop in the bag, for, as everyone knew, time was of the essence, Fitzgerald's bar being neatly across the road.

Men and machines refreshed and watered, they set out to begin the real battle; while the line from Tralee was undulating and twisty, that westwards was of a very different character. Immediately the junction was left behind the train arrived at the foot of the celebrated Glenagalt Bank, certainly the most formidable in Ireland and probably unsurpassed in length and severity anywhere in the British Isles. The rails climbed from almost sea level to a height of 680ft in just under four miles, with ruling gradients of 1 in 30 and 1 in 31. It was had enough when maintenance was good but with wet grass lying over the rails life could become difficult in the extreme.

It would be 1pm before the new single line token was collected and once more whistle answered whistle, two chimneys erupted smoke and steam simultaneously like active volcanoes and they were away. Speed varied between 5 and 15mph depending on adhesion and, accompanied by the slow syncopated rhythm of the two locomotives the train set off on stage two of its journey. Slowly, like a great horned snake it heaved its way up, hampered by more straying sheep, now a foot above the road, now in a shallow cutting to even out the gradient: some half an hour later it creaked to a brief stop at the summit alongside Glenagalt platform. The next crossing point – though there was nothing to cross any longer (unless they ran three specials) – would be Annascaul.

From there the line twisted and turned following each indentation of the hillside and all the time descending in longer stretches of 1 in 29/30. Footplate passengers glanced at the vacuum gauge for reassurance, remembering the fitter back at Tralee tinkering with the hose coupling rubbers to cure the worst of the leakage As the train came writhing down the hill with the weatherbeaten cattle trucks wagging behind the engines there was still the sheep hazard to contend with; this was met by firm brake applications, open drain cocks and the squeal of flanges. The temporary panic over, gravity once more took charge and the train bowled down the bank at an unnerving 25–30mph, the engines nosing their way along the rusty grass-grown track. Soon the line came into Gleann an Scail where the legendary hero Cuchulainn fought his great battle with the giant and the countryside was strewn with the huge rocks they hurled in their combat. By now most of the coal was away from under the feet in the cabs and after a total of four road crossings, and with a last long whistle the train shot under an arch of trees and dropped down into the station at Annascaul. The water tank here was at the end of a small bridge over a stream at the Dingle end of the station and beyond was a level crossing which was blocked for the 20 minute stop. Men and machines once more refreshed themselves, superintended by the stationmaster sent down for the day by bus from Tralee. A minor traffic jam of lorries and donkey carts built up slowly to mark the importance of the occasion.

Right out of Annascaul the climb began at 1 in 32; 8T's fireman mopped his brow, took a long swig from his can and proceeded to lay a smoke screen over the 12ft high fuschia hedges in readiness for the slog. For the four miles up to Garrynadur the railway swung from the road with its vicious hairpin bends impossible to follow. Up here the track seemed less overgrown and with sharp exhausts and rhythmic kicks of the reversing wheel against its restraining chain 8T and its helper made their way towards the summit. Here was the ganger's house, the probable explanation for the better track; after a wave from his daughter, the train was off on a repetition of the descent from Glenagalt until grinding brakes brought it to a stop on the last few yards of the 1 in 29 (nominal) gradient.

Just ahead lay Lispole viaduct, the line's major engineering work; it was a spidery two span structure with stone approach arches and the 1 in 29 finished at the start of the steel spans. Light construction plus 60 years of salt winds off the Atlantic had taken their toll and, since as long back as 1929 there had been a prohibition on two locomotives crossing the girders at the same time. So they uncoupled, with 8T going across light and 1T rolling the train over very gently. Safely reunited they were off again over five more miles of undulating track alongside the long straight road to Dingle: farmers with horse drawn carts covered the heads of their animals with coats as the train approached. Then, turning across the road once more they swung

23

into a nasty rise in a shallow cutting between stone walls, grass lying deep on the track, the bottom corner of the motion plate cutting a swathe in the vegetation; they were down to a walking pace before levelling off and drifting down into Dingle. Behind the station yard lay the landlocked harbour, fishing boats loafing against the quay, answering with its tranquillity the furious efforts to reach it. It had taken just four hours from leaving Tralee. The enginemen disposed of some of the stock to the cattle bank for loading the next day, turned the engines, cleaned the fires and banked them for the night then moved the remaining briquettes into the cabs. The stiff but invigorated footplate passenger went off to Benners Hotel for a meal (Would you like fresh salmon or trout – or are you meat eaters?) and a heavy night in the bar on fresh Guinness.

The crews looked distinctly jaded next morning, all except Hanlon, who had been at home. Indeed 1T's fireman was nowhere to be found but with help from the other Side of the Water the train was made up. It was warm with little breeze and the flies descended in swarms as the cattle pens became slippery underfoot, but finally the train, made up of an empty coal wagon, 11 loaded cattle trucks with no animals down, and the van, was ready. By 12.15 1T's fireman was still absent; there was a conference between drivers and a very prolonged whistle then it was decided to go and 'sure he'll catch us up before long.' So it proved; after the train had moved on to the long straight by the side of the road, a Post Office van overtook it and stopped beyond. Out tumbled the fireman, obviously with a king sized hangover and was dragged aboard by willing hands. The enthusiast did more of the firing than the rightful fireman for the rest of the trip.

As the train swung off the roadside at Lispole platform the Englishman waited to see how the two engines would tackle the climb at 1 in 29 from a standing start. He need not have wondered. As the viaduct came into view both were opened well out and hit the spans doubleheaded at fully 20mph to rush the bank. But they made it all right and slogged up to Garrynadur and thence down to the water tank at Annascaul.

On the roadside beyond there was a fair bit of trouble with slipping; 8T carried a large box of sand which meant everyone bar the drivers taking it in turns to be out sprinkling the rails by hand. It was touch and go at times and infuriating to be caught up and overtaken by a red faced elderly man on a bicycle. So to Glenagalt and the statutory stop at the summit, an anxious glance at the vacuum gauge and off down the hill to Castlegregory Junction. Below the 'new' bridge over the Fingles Burn there was a flock of sheep grazing on the line. Brakes hard on, whistle and yells: all cleared except one which was hit with a sickening thud and then thrown clear. The guard came up at the junction and asked 'Why did ye not stop and pick it up?' They could no more have stopped than fly to the moon. More water, more refreshment and out on to the last lap to make a slow but by now weary way to the Tralee streets and the deserted narrow gauge station at 4.30pm. The journey was over and the Grand Hotel's monumental

24

high tea beckoned.

Though the Tralee & Dingle was, perhaps, the most exciting of Ireland's narrow gauge railways it was a comparatively short line; those in search of narrow gauge networks had to trek northwards to Donegal. Here were two railways of some size, connected by a short spur at Letterkenny and by the Port and Harbour Commissioners' line at Londonderry. They were the Londonderry & Lough Swilly Railway and the County Donegal Railways Joint Committee. The former ultimately rejected transport by rail, embarked on the purchase of buses, bought out all competitors and eventually replaced its railway workings by road services. The latter, probably because it was owned by two large railway companies (the Great Northern of Ireland and the LMS), decided to keep going; it did so by eliminating steam from all but freight and excursion services with the introduction of what were virtually railbuses to suit local needs. Diesel traction by these railbuses began in 1931. Even as late as the 1950s it was a relief to turn from the spectacle of closed and dying narrow gauge railways to the bustling and efficient County Donegal with its route mileage still verging on 100. By then road competition had already set in and it really was make do and mend; these were the years which ate into the contingency fund, but it was a fight to the death with no apparent thought of surrender. One might deplore the replacement of steam, but the system lived by the aid of this new power and that was better than the alternative of no railway at all. Steam was still there on the more or less regular heavy goods trains and on the summer specials to the sea at Ballyshannon; it was to see these that the faithful came to Stranorlar. They stayed at the hotel used and recommended by the line's General Manager, Barney Curran, over the river at Ballybofey where the food was attuned to the hearty appetites of outdoor life. It was, however, even then, a meeting place for the Republican movement and asides that 'it might be best if ye didn't come back too early now' were not unknown

The last year was 1959. Even then there was a regular steam goods service on the Strabane and Letterkenny section and also over the Finn Valley to Stranorlar, occasionally extended to Donegal, though after 1957 the railcars could usually cope with the traffic beyond that point. Officially these steam trains were freight only but the passenger brake on the rear carried a favoured few. With luck the Finn Valley goods would go on over the bare and rugged terrain of the West Donegal, the exhaust slowing as they took the bank towards Meenglas and the climb to Barnesmore. Usually it was with one of the smaller 2–6–4 tanks *Drumboe* or *Meenglas* but sometimes the larger *Blanche* or even the older 4–6–4 tank *Erne*. On the days that they took an abbreviated train to Killybegs the duty was an exacting one, with a late evening arrival followed by an early start back the next morning in time to pick up the schedule of the next round trip at Stranorlar, perhaps with the same engine. This was tough going for the ageing McMenamin brothers Jim and Frank, as they were the only Stranorlar men left; during the winter months the train crew never saw Killybegs by day for they arrived and left during the long

*Stranorlar station and yard, County Donegal Railways Joint Committee, in August 1957. In the background is the station with a coach in the east end bay platform. Note the imposing clock tower which was over the arch into the gents' lavatory. On the left is the Baltic tank No 14* Erne *dating from 1904, while on the right is a modern (1936) diesel railcar No 18 and behind it a red painted van denoting its use as a railcar trailer.*
P.B. Whitehouse

hours of darkness.

In a way the Killybegs line, with its Atlantic shore, could almost have been called the Donegal's equivalent of the Lough Swilly's Burtonport Extension, less wild maybe and actually following the shores of Donegal Bay. Here the coastline consisted of a series of deep inlets between lofty headlands jutting far out into the sea with the railway line crossing over the spines making it a hard road to work, the engines labouring on gradients as steep as 1 in 41. Although everything was far superior in construction and maintenance to the Tralee & Dingle it meant panting climbs and rocketing descents with squealing flanges lurching round the sharp curves in the manner of a fairground helter skelter.

But it was summer Bank Holiday times that provided the last great occasions for steam and even in the later years the crowds were heavy both from Strabane and Stranorlar. Generally it was a happy cheerful throng and bottles were out and opened early. Over a good dinner the normally quiet Barney Curran would reminisce and once told the

THE
COUNTY DONEGAL RAILWAYS
(JOINT COMMITTEE.)

No. 101 ISSUE.

## WORKING TIME TABLE

(For use of Committee's Staff only)

AS

From SUNDAY, 29th JUNE, 1958

until further notice.

M—Rail Car Service.     S—Steam Train.

No Special Train, Engine or Motor must be allowed to run over the Line without authority from the Manager's Office, and before any such Special is despatched, the Station Masters concerned must see that complete arrangements are made for its safe working, and that of any other Train or Trains which it may have to precede, cross or follow. Station Masters must see that the E.T.S. arrangements and signalling of Trains are carried out, and that a copy of the Special Train Notice is sent to gatekeepers under their supervision. A single bar thus —— denotes the station appointed for a train to cross another travelling in the opposite direction.

**REMEMBER !**

It is well for each Member of this Railway to bear in mind that goodwill based upon years of conscientious effort may be entirely destroyed by a moment's carelessness or indifference toward a customer.

---

THE COUNTY DONEGAL RAILWAYS
(JOINT COMMITTEE)

TELEGRAMS "CURRAN, BALLYBOFEY"
PHONE: BALLYBOFEY 8
B. L. CURRAN,
MANAGER AND SECRETARY

MANAGER'S OFFICE,
STRANORLAR,
CO. DONEGAL

This is to authorize Mr. P. B. Whitehouse to travel on the footplate of 9-5 p.m. Donegal to Stranorlar today

B. Curran
5/8/1957

---

story of the man who joined the excursion from Strabane already, as the Irish would put it, the better for drink, and by the time the train had reached Stranorlar, the line's headquarters, he was proving a bit of a nuisance Curran had him out and put him on the engine (it was the 2–6–4 tank *Lydia* where there was room enough) with strict instructions to the engine crew that he was to be kept in front of the fire. The day was hot and by the time they had fought their way up the bank and run down through the Barnesmore Gap with the firehole door open he had had enough, so they put him off at Donegal and never had any more trouble.

The last excursion ran on August Bank Holiday Monday 1959 and, as in previous years, there were two trains using the entire available stock patched up and gathered together for the occasion, including the saloon The heavier train from Strabane ran with *Blanche* and eleven coaches while the second, with seven, followed from Stranorlar crewed by the McMenamin brothers. Both were packed to the doors. During the long wait at Ballyshannon while the crowds were enjoying the sun at Bundoran there was some consultation over *Blanche*'s steaming and it was decided that *Meenglas* would take the main train home to Strabane.

In the event, the very last excursion of all was hauled by *Blanche*. The journey from Ballyshannon to Donegal was taken first with a stop at Rossnowlagh to pick up a further crowd of passengers, and as the sun lowered itself into the west they ran into the platform at Donegal. In a moment Frank McMenamin had eased up, his brother Jim uncoupled, and they were away over the crossing to back on to the water column and to clean the fire in readiness for the climb ahead. Back then on to the other end of the train, couple up and connect the vacuum 'bag' and they were away, *Blanche* vomiting black

27

*The last return Strabane excursion from Ballyshannon and Donegal climbs up through the Barnesmore Gap with a heavy train of ten coaches and a bogie van on August Bank Holiday Monday 1959. The engine is 2-6-4 tank No 4* Meenglass *painted geranium red, and the coaches in red and cream are mostly of CDRJC origin. The exceptions are vehicles 4, 5 and 6 which are ex LMS built specially in 1928 in Midland style as corridor stock for the 3ft 0in gauge boat trains between Larne and Ballymena before construction of the Greenisland loop. They were made redundant on the closure of the Ballycastle branch (to which they had been transferred) in 1950.*
P.B. Whitehouse

smoke as the red and cream train disappeared away from the fading sun.

From Donegal the line rose slowly but steadily towards the Blue Stack Mountains, the gradient becoming steeper all the time towards the crossing loop and staff section point at Lough Eske. Two shovelfuls at the front of the box, and another in the middle, pause, two at the back, pause, front again, pause, and so it went on, opening and closing the firebox door after each shovelful. Jim was using a fairly light fire and the needle kept steady in the gauge, a plume of steam and smoke dropping away behind the train.

Over the road crossing at Lough Eske the more scenic section of the climb began; the character of the line changed completely as they set off round the curve towards the lower reach of hills and away from the road. There was a slight respite here as the gradient eased a little allowing the fire to be checked and the boiler topped up as they crossed under the road by Barnesmore Halt platform. Here the long stretch of 1 in 60 began and the next three miles was one of the most spectacular and dramatic sections of any Irish railway, the line clinging to the slopes high up above the winding river and road from which the train appeared to be a slow moving model against the mountainous landscape. At the summit rail and road came together

28

and a small crowd waited to pay its respects as *Blanche* made her way along the high embankment, her crowded train behind her. A few minutes more and they were under Derg bridge and making their way alongside the silver waters of Lough Mourne. Once away from the road the descent began, again at 1 in 60, and for the next five miles the McMenamins took it easy, keeping their eyes on the darkness in front. All too soon the lights of Stranorlar came into view and air was allowed into the train pipe; round the curve and over the river they came, the miniature train staff was handed to Pat Monteith at Stranorlar West Box and they drew to a halt at the east end of the platform with its clock tower neatly over the gents' lavatory. The crowd swarmed off into the darkness and silence descended.

The last steam engine to work the West Donegal section was the 54-year-old Baltic tank No 14, *Erne*, manned as usual by the McMenamins, this time with Jim driving and Frank firing to him. Old Frank was put off driving towards the end as he failed to pass the medical but, even so, the two brothers continued to work as before, Jim driving the engine through Stranorlar just in case someone was watching; once out of sight they went back to their former jobs. It was the last day but one, 30 December 1959, and Ballyshannon was making sure that it got its supplies as cheap as possible, so they left Strabane with a long train. In the evening they set off from Stranorlar, having waited for the last railcar to come over the long section from Lough Eske, and they headed for the Barnesmore Gap in the winter's darkness, the slow heavy beat carrying across the quiet night into the homes of many who had spent their lives in the service of the railway.

They worked back on the morning of New Year's Eve, but it was not the end yet. The final run out of Killybegs was made by railcar No 12 which was scheduled to run right through to Strabane in accordance with normal practice, but this proved to be an exceptional day. As the evening drew on and the last mails had gone down to Strabane in railcar No 16 the crowds began to turn up in force at Stranorlar and it became clear that no railcar would be able to cope with the traffic, so Barney Curran decided that the last passenger train of all would be with steam. This was made up of five coaches and 2–6–4 tank No 5 *Drumboe* manned by the only available crew – the McMenamins; they left 20min late and went into the drizzling darkness to a chorus of exploding detonators. When they arrived back at Stranorlar both the brothers were actually in tears, overcome by emotion,, for this really was the end, and a lifetime's work on the railway was finished. The next day, New Year's Day 1960, Frank left the service; Jim was kept on as a lorry loader but as he said, it will never be the same again.

# CHAPTER ONE
# NARROW-GAUGE ORIGINS

The coal-cart, or Stephenson, gauge of railways, 5ft or a little less, is very ancient since it grew out of the traditional distance between the wheels of carts in Roman times. Plenty of archaeological evidence exists in Mediterranean lands, mainly in the form of ruts worn into the rock, or the pavements of old roads, to show that this dimension has hardly varied in 2000 years. Railways themselves are nothing like as old as this, if the distinction rests in the pathway being prepared not only to carry the weight of the wheel, but also to guide it. In this form, the primitive ancestor of the railway seems to have come into existence a little over 400 years ago. In the darkness of a mediaeval mine tunnel, with little room on each side and abrupt curves to follow the vein or lode of coal or ore, automatic steering of the cars and wagons used to bring out spoil was found very useful. It so happens that the oldest illustration to show such a vehicle, in the *De Re Metallica* of Agricola, published in 1556, proves quite clearly that its wheels were something like 2ft apart.

This would seem to indicate that the narrow-gauge railway has an ancestry every bit as old as that of the standard-gauge, while the broad gauge is a definite Johnny-come-lately, not appearing in fact until some time after the steam locomotive. But Agricola's mine truck pre-dates the flange, whether applied to the wheel or the rail, for it was guided by a peg running along a slot. During the 17th century the railway began to emerge from the tunnels and byways of mines and workshops, and strike across open country. Usually its destination was the nearest navigable water, since long-distance movement of heavy loads was only feasible in ships or canal or river boats. By the late 18th century there were two rival species of railway (slotways having already disappeared). The older was the 'edge railway', on which each wheel of a pair on the same axle had a single flange, running along the edge of a plain squared rail, at first of wood and later of iron. More recent was the 'plateway', on which the wheels were narrow and unflanged, running along the flat of an iron plate, one edge of which carried a raised lip or flange to provide guidance. The plateway had seemed like a good idea because it could be used by wheels also able to run on ordinary roads; in practice though it was found that this could not be achieved, since friction was too great unless the wheel tread was made so narrow that it damaged any stone or gravel surface it ran on. In 1797 John Curr described a system of 2ft gauge plateways which then existed in the coal districts of Nottinghamshire and South Yorkshire, in which

automatic guidance through switches at the entrance to passing loops on single line was achieved by canting the track by 2in and so throwing the wheel in the desired direction without having to use any moving parts.

As history records, however, it was the standard-gauge edge railway that caught on and spread widely, especially with the development of steam traction. It is worth pointing out, though, that there is debatable ground even here; the first commercially successful use of steam locomotives, on the Middleton Railway near Leeds from 1812, was on rails 4ft apart, a track gauge rather wide to be described as narrow, but definitely narrower than standard. In general the narrow-gauge railway remained the poor sister, kept out of sight and inconspicuous, although there was a fair mileage of it by 1850, for instance in South Wales. There, while the network of over 100 miles of 4ft 4in gauge horse-drawn plateways in the Western Valleys above Newport was converted to standard-gauge railways in 1849 (marking the end of the last major plateway system), the 3ft 4in gauge system of edge railways in the Eastern Valleys, of about half the length, remained for some years longer.

The area in Britain most closely associated with narrow gauge

*Pointwork for the double-flanged system of internal tramways in the Oakeley Quarries, Blaenau Festiniog, in 1953. All trackwork is complete and in full working order, though one rail leading to the siding on the extreme right is hidden away! But changing the points was a matter of some complexity.*
J.B. Snell

31

One of the narrow-gauge steam engines in use at Crewe Works London & North Western Railway, Billy *of July 1875 proudly displayed adjacent to a Crewe type 2–4–0 and a Ramsbottom 2–4–0 both sporting Fancis Webb's chimneys. The gauge is 1ft 6in.* By courtesy of the National Railway Museum

railways was, and remains, North Wales, where they first were used, as they had been in England, in connection with mineral workings. From 1801 until the steam railway arrived in the area in mid-century the valleys of Snowdonia came to be laced with a series of narrow-gauge lines linking the various quarries with tidewater at a number of tiny ports. By an accident of history they came to figure much more prominently in the record than the many older mining and industrial lines in England and in South Wales, simply because one of them, the Festiniog, became the first steam-powered narrow-gauge railway to offer its services to the public as a common carrier of freight and passenger traffic. All others until then had been private lines, used only for the purposes of their owners. The Festiniog is also often said to be the first narrow-gauge line to use steam locomotives, but this is not true. It was certainly the first to run steam-hauled public passenger trains, in 1865; but Zerah Colburn's book *Locomotive Engineering* published in 1864, listed a number of earlier examples of narrow-gauge steam traction. The Neath Abbey Ironworks, in South Wales, built a 6¾-ton engine of 2ft 8½in gauge for its own use, and displayed it at the 1862 International Exhibition. A 2ft 6in gauge line at the Willenhall Furnaces, in Staffordshire, 1½ miles long and with 1 in 30 gradient, had several 8-ton 0–4–0Ts at work by that time. The London & North Western Railway put the first locomotive, the 2½-ton *Tiny* into service on its 18in gauge tramway at Crewe Works in 1862, while the previous year Isaac W. Boulton built a 3½-ton geared engine for a mile-long 2ft gauge line near Wigan, which had a 1 in 50 gradient and a rathole of a tunnel only 6ft 6in in diameter. All these lines and locomotives were, of course, industrial. It was the demonstration at Portmadoc that narrow-gauge steam railways could be used for ordinary public commercial traffic that made news, not the mere fact that small locomotives were practical.

For the next 10 or 15 years the Festiniog became world-famous, as an exemplar of the ideas of such propagandists as its Manager, Charles Spooner, and the locomotive designer Robert Fairlie. The case they argued ran as follows. There was no purpose in proposing

any alteration to the gauge of any existing railway (although, as a matter of fact, it would have been possible and profitable to work even such a heavy traffic as was then carried on some of the main lines by the narrow gauge). Indeed they would even agree that in some ways the Festiniog line was *too* narrow, and in particular, too tightly limited by clearances designed to pass horses and not loco-motives. The great and important advantage the narrow gauge possessed was just that it could be built more cheaply. The trains were smaller and therefore less costly, and so were the bridges; but above all the cost of the earthworks and rock-splitting, very great in those pick-and-shovel days, could be reduced considerably, partly because the cuttings and embankments could be narrower but mainly because the narrow gauge line could turn sharper curves, and therefore follow the contours more closely through hilly districts. This real reduction in first cost might well make it possible, because only in this way could it be economic to build rail-ways to places which would otherwise have to do without. In fact the question was just the one Fairlie used for the title of a book: *Railways or No Railways*. No particular force with which the argu-ment could he applied to projects to build lines to develop remote places, then just beginning to be settled and opened up, was widely

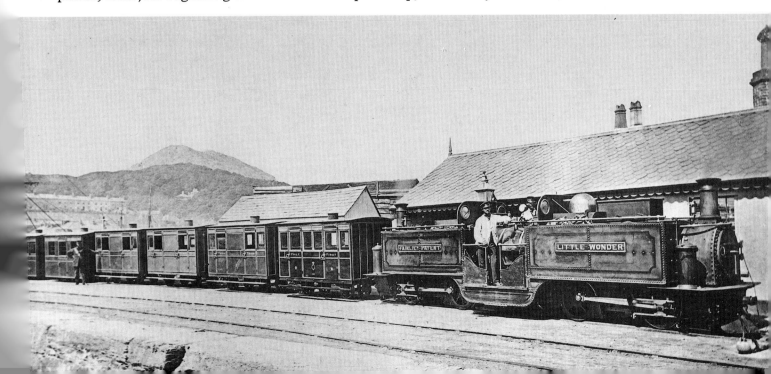

appreciated, and it was in large part due to the example of the Festiniog that railways of gauges around 3ft, 1 metre, or 3ft 6in, came to be built on a huge scale in such places as America, Japan, India, Southern Africa, and Australasia.

The Spooner-Fairlie doctrine had the great merit of being calculable and scientific. The actual savings in terms of cubic yards of rock to be shifted, tonnage of iron required, and cash needed to pay for it all, could he worked out accurately in every case. There was never again any need to resort to the leap-in-the-dark school of engineering, of which perhaps the classic example was the Royal Commission in 1845 which settled the question of what gauge the railways of Ireland should be, by pooling the recommendations of those they consulted and coming up with 5ft 3in. It became possible to decide the question of how to build a new railway rationally. After 1865 no further broad gauge systems were established anywhere in the world, and only those which already existed continued (though a few were converted to narrow). Narrow-gauge public railway construction, on the other hand, boomed. The lines built could he divided into two classes. Both had in common the fact that they originally served areas where it was not thought that enough traffic would exist to justify standard gauge; in other respects they followed very different lines of development.

Into the first category fall those lines which have become national systems. The railways of southern and central Africa, much of Asia, Australasia, and South America, now outrank many standard or broad-gauge undertakings in density of traffic, size of equipment, and even speed. They have gone beyond Spooner and Fairlie and demonstrate that in fact the distance between the rails is a pretty unimportant matter, just so long as it is constant throughout every national network; any figure from 3ft to 5ft 6in will do admirably. Much more important is the question of good management, sound design, and proper maintenance. A ramshackle broad-gauge line is a loveless thing, and its greater cost makes the achievement of proper standards rather more difficult. South Africa and Japan (on the older, principal, network) run better and faster trains than Ireland or the Argentine, sunk in their broad-gauge darkness; maximum speeds and loads in Finland and New Zealand are much the same, since each country can afford approximately the same standard of equipment and this cancels out the 18in difference between their gauges. There are, of course, no railways in this category in Britain, and indeed few in Europe, though the metre-gauge networks in northern Spain and south-eastern Switzerland, even if they are not national, are certainly regional and reach these main-line standards.

The second category consists of those lines which were built in light-traffic areas to serve as feeders to national systems of a different gauge. Some of the more successful examples ultimately widened their tracks and became part of the national network. Some of the once vast narrow-gauge mileage in North America, for example, was converted in this way. Other lines reduced the inconvenience of the break-of-gauge by having special trucks on one to carry the vehicles of the other; there were four examples of this altogether in the British Isles, though many more in Europe.

All the British and Irish narrow-gauge lines, public and private, fell into the second category, except that some of the industrial and agricultural lines were not in fact primarily feeders to the national system, but self-contained because the traffic they carried did not have to be transferred to another train to complete its journey. This gave them the advantage that they did not have to face the cost and confusion of the break of gauge, which was one factor which ultimately sank most of the others. But there were other problems too.

In fact the trouble was that however correct and powerful the Spooner and Fairlie arguments for narrow-gauge feeder lines were a hundred years ago, times changed. Then, the situation was that railways were the only practical form of inland transport, and people were prepared to build them, even when they would certainly be unprofitable because they would nevertheless be economic; the

*Before the present day expansion and improvement of Britain's road system and the growth of the powerful motor tractor and lorry, narrow-gauge mineral and quarry railways abounded. Typical of these were the iron ore lines of the Midlands, exemplified here by the 3ft 0in gauge Kettering Ironstone system. This photograph, taken in August 1961, shows Kettering Furnaces No 8 (Manning, Wardle 1675/06) drawing a train of ore out of the quarry. The line closed in 1962. G.D. King*

*A new tourist railway now runs over the track bed of a section of the old Dinorwic Railway main (4ft 0in) gauge line from Llanberis. The track has been laid to the 2ft 0in gauge using ex quarry 0-4-0 saddle tank* Dolbadarn *albeit rebuilt with weather protection for the crew. The train in this photograph is at the Llanberis terminus adjacent to what is now Quarry Museum.* C.M. Whitehouse.

alternative was to continue to rely on the horse and cart. A narrow-gauge line would sometimes be preferable because it was less unprofitable, though since by the 1860s most of the promising parts of Britain had already been reached by the standard gauge, only the unpromising parts were left for the narrow and so the prospects of almost all the public British narrow-gauge lines were, even at the start, poor. With the rise of the internal combustion engine and the revival of road transport, they got worse.

The cards were further stacked by an alteration in relative costs. Spooner and Fairlie could claim correctly enough that a narrow-gauge train was cheaper to operate than a standard-gauge one, directly in pence per ton-mile carried. A Festiniog articulated locomotive hauled about the same payload, and needed the same number of men in a train crew, as a typical main line freight of the period; but the smaller narrow-gauge stock represented less initial outlay, needed less fuel to propel it, and cost less to repair. But the narrow-gauge locomotives used in Britain hardly increased in power thereafter, while main-line locomotives had become incomparably more powerful even before the steam era ended. The fuel cost advantage may have remained with the narrow gauge, but wage costs became much more important. With the great increase in payload on the standard gauge, the balance of total cost per ton-mile shifted moved very much to the disadvantage of the narrow gauge.

With the industrial lines, another factor applied. The enormous variety of rubber-tyred or road-using mechanical handling equipment in use nowadays, which began with the steam shovel and dragline excavator during the nineteenth century and now includes the ubiquitous fork-lift truck, the mobile crane, and a plethora of more specialised equipment, has in almost every case provided a better and cheaper means of doing the work the industrial, contractor's, or mining railway used to do.

The upshot has been that almost all the narrow-gauge lines have disappeared. But this does not prove any weakness in the original concept, because pretty well all the comparable standard-gauge lines have now gone too, whether they were public railways of the rural branch line type or industrials. The survival of any railway in Britain, other than a busy trunk route or one with a heavy local traffic, is now almost the exception. And a new factor has grown up in the last half-century which has enabled the remaining narrow-gauge public lines to survive, in fact to become more active and healthy than perhaps they ever were in the old days. This is the fact that the public have taken to them not as transport so much as entertainment; they are simply fun to ride on. They earn their living by carrying crowds of happy holidaymakers. And why not? It is as real and genuine a business as any other, and it demands at least as high a standard of professional performance to achieve success.

*One of England's largest narrow gauge systems, if not the largest, was the network of tramways based on Birmingham and the Black Country. In late Victorian and Edwardian days the trams were steam hauled. A Kitson locomotive and trailer are shown here ascending Park Road, Moseley, Birmingham on the King's Heath service about 1900.*
Millbrook House Collection

# CHAPTER TWO
# ENGLAND, SCOTLAND, AND THE ISLE OF MAN

If one is careful to make exact definitions, one can say accurately enough that the fully-fledged public narrow-gauge railway never made much of an appearance in Britain outside Wales, for the main reason that both England and Scotland were by the last quarter of the 19th century very liberally endowed with standard-gauge passenger-carrying lines, to practically every place where enough traffic offered to make them pay plus many where it did not. Only a few narrow-gauge concerns thus ever found enough of a foothold to get built on; most were very short and only two managed routes over 10 miles long. However, on each side of the narrowest definition matters were otherwise. Of the enormous number of urban and suburban tramways built, and the much smaller number of rural roadside tramways, there was a considerable amount of narrow-gauge mileage, often originally steam-worked, the very substantial 3ft 6in gauge network around Birmingham being a case in point. While of the equally large number of mining and industrial railways never open to the public, a high proportion also were of narrow gauge. Space will not allow even the barest justice to be done to either of these categories of railway, except to say that by the 1870s they were already numerous.

In fact the first public narrow-gauge railway in Britain outside Wales was not in Britain but the Isle of Man, where the break-of-gauge drawback did not apply as there were no other railways at all. The 11½-mile line from Douglas, the capital of the island, to Peel on the opposite coast, was opened on the 3ft gauge in 1873 and by 1886 the island's steam railway system had reached its full extent of 46 route-miles. The Isle of Man Railway was for a long time, indeed into the 1950s, successful and prosperous, carrying passengers and freight all year round using a fleet of locomotives and rolling stock which was enlarged as traffic grew but which hardly changed in design for 80 years. The original four-wheeled coaches were replaced by bogie stock (often with two old bodies mounted together on a new long frame), the locomotives got a little bigger between 1873 and 1926, but all continued to exist (and indeed officially still do, though some have been evaporated or condensed into practical non-existence by cannibalisation in recent years) though all but one of the 16 were fundamentally of the same design. Together with the rival Manx Electric, an 18-mile and non-connected concern with its own route also 3ft gauge up the other side of the island from Douglas to Ramsey, plus the 3ft 6in gauge

*Manx Northern Railway 0–6–0 tank No 4* Caledonia *with a special train of six-wheeled stock at Foxdale terminus; the engine is in MNR livery and has come chimney first out of Ramsey. There is no platform and the early signals are just visible at the rear of the train. This was the occasion of the opening of the Foxdale branch, Monday 16 August 1886.* Manx Museum

*Isle of Man Railway Beyer Peacock 2–4–0T No 2* Derby *waits at Ramsey station with the 6.15pm to Douglas on 16 May 1927 with both driver and fireman in attendance.* A.W. Croughton

Douglas Terminus, Isle of Man Railway in its last years of operation as a complete system. The locomotive is Beyer Peacock 2–4–0 tank No 10 G.H. Wood (4662/05). C.M. Whitehouse

Manx Electric Railway electric car and trailer at Douglas in 1968. Undeniably a tramway system this double-track line is the most spectacular of all the Island's railways and now the only rail route to Ramsey. P.B. Whitehouse

electric line up Snaefell, which both also remained almost unchallenged from their openings in the 1890s, the Manx railways made a most remarkable example of antique railway operation for a very long time indeed. By about 1960, however, road transport had effectively taken over all the freight business and most of the passenger traffic as well apart from the summer visitors, and things began to slip. The electric lines have survived intact, with the aid of the Manx government; the steam railway after some remarkable ups and downs and a period of complete closure in the 1970s has now been reduced to the 15½-mile Port Erin line only, but in character the extraordinary originality of both systems remains pretty well intact. Now both concerns are under the same government management, but still form one of the most successful and interesting examples of railway preservation anywhere, helped in this of course by the island's comparative isolation.

In its heyday, the Isle of Man Railway had perhaps more of the fully-fledged main-line railway atmosphere about it than any other British (but not Irish) narrow-gauge system. Its terminus at Douglas was a substantial affair with good buildings and covered platforms; the whole line was fully signalled, even if the signals themselves were antediluvian. The two single lines, to Port Erin and to Peel and Ramsey, disappeared side by side like a proper double track. There was a goods yard, a substantial locomotive shed, and a considerable and a fully-equipped works, and there was a good, frequent, train service on all lines throughout the year. The sharp-eyed might notice that even if the steam heating pipes were coupled up in winter, the vacuum brake pipes never were, and trains stopped slowly and gently only on the fireman's handbrake, in contravention of the Regulation of Railways Act 1889; but that was a mainland statute and nobody took the goings-on at Westminster very seriously. There was even a set of snowploughs for winter use, plus one very large plough attached to the rarest locomotive of all, the solitary 0–6–0T *Caledonia* which since the end of the lead mines at Foxdale years earlier had been kept in reserve to handle only the rarest and severest snowfalls, emerging two or three times every decade. Shortly after 1945 the chairman of the company announced at an annual meeting that some new locomotives were at last to be obtained; but it never happened, and it was sad instead to see the slow decline of the system from about 1950 onwards, a process repeated later on a much larger scale on the mainland. It was seen at first by the curtailment of services so that the whole railway, with its numerous signalmen and level crossing keepers, could be operated during a single shift each day. Despite this, up to the end of year-round operation, stacks of parcels used to be unloaded from elderly red motor vans at Douglas station and piled onto the trains every morning, to be taken off later at places like Port St Mary and loaded into remarkably similar and equally ancient motor vans again for final delivery. Occasionally the unworthy thought occurred, that it was the same red motor van in each case, but photographic evidence is not conclusive of this.

IMPORTANT TO VISITORS

# Manx Electric Railway

The Direct Coast Route to LAXEY AND RAMSEY

*A Continuous Panorama of Mountain, Glen and Marine Scenery*

★ 2 Day Excursion

'ROVER'
TICKET 16/-

ANYWHERE . . ANYTIME

( *Within Seven Days of Date of Issue* )

★ ★ INCLUDING ONE RETURN JOURNEY TO ★ ★

SUMMIT OF SNAEFELL
MOUNTAIN

Don't miss this golden
opportunity to see
MANXLAND'S FINEST SCENERY!

ASK FOR AN M.E.R. 'ROVER' TICKET

TICKETS obtainable at the SEFTON BOOKING OFFICE
DERBY CASTLE STATION, LAXEY and RAMSEY

1 Strathallan Crescent,
Douglas.     H. GILMORE, General Manager.
Strickett - Printer - Ramsey.

*Manx electric railway leaflet*

*A rare photograph of a 3ft 0in gauge Ravenglass & Eskdale Railway passenger train. The scene is Ravenglass station with the 0–6–0 tank* Devon *and two four-wheeled coaches, the leading vehicle being all first class; note the smoking notice above the window of the compartment adjacent to the engine. Oil lamps are evident as is the lack of any form of continuous braking. The date is sometime in the 1890s. By courtesy of National Railway Museum*

The Manx Electric Railway firmly called itself a railway; indeed it is one, even if the trains it operates are equally undeniably trams. Double track throughout, it never actually runs in the public road, and for its whole length is either on a reserved formation at the roadside or, rather more often, on its own independent right-of-way. Its curves and gradients are certainly tramway-like, and it has no signals except for some automatic ones at level crossings (put in years earlier than anything similar on the mainland); its operating practices are again tram-like and not railway-like (in other words, flexible, with extra trips run at the drop of a hat when business offers). But somehow it has the feel of a proper railway. The railway enthusiast often undervalues it in comparison with the steam railway, quite wrongly, since both are very fine examples of their kind, but the Electric nowadays rather the rarer of the pair, and certainly scenically much the more spectacular.

The first public narrow-gauge railway in England was another 3ft gauge concern, the Ravenglass & Eskdale, 6¾ miles long and opened in 1875. Like some of the Welsh lines, its main justification was mineral traffic, in this case haematite ore from various small workings around Boot, at the head of Eskdale in the Lake District, though general public traffic was also intended to be handled from the outset. Unlike most mineral lines, however, it had a substantial length of adverse gradient against the generally descending load, where it climbed out of Eskdale and into Miterdale in order to reach the Furness Railway connection at Ravenglass, and so its two locomotives were turned the opposite way round to those on similar lines so that they could tackle this heavy working chimney first. Alas for such careful calculations; the ore traffic never amounted to anything productive of heavy working. The R&ER was soon bankrupt, but staggered on gently for 30 years or so on the few crumbs of general business that came its way, falling slowly to pieces and being embarrassed once each August Bank Holiday by vast crowds of passengers. Little known at first in its remote and lovely valleys, the Eskdale was becoming quite famous as a bucolic mechanical curiosity, rather like the Talyllyn 40 years later, when debts and dilapidations finally forced its closure, to passengers in 1908 and at last to freight in 1913. In those days, however, death was not

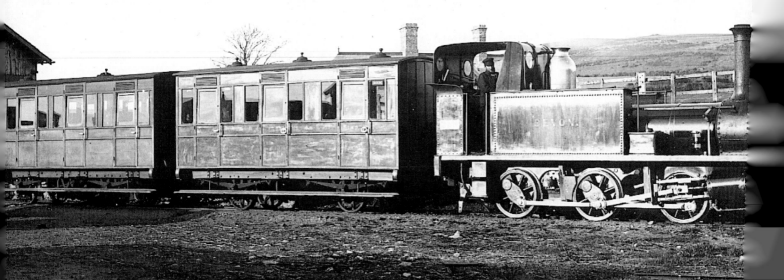

*Ravenglass station in 1927. Davey Paxman 2–8–2* River Esk *waits with a short train under the overall roof. The locomotive was built in 1923 and is still in service today. The roof was removed and the track layout rearranged the following winter. A.W. Croughton*

always permanent.

The next line was the third and last public 3ft gauge line in Britain, and one which has long passed into folklore. The 8½-mile long Southwold Railway, opened in 1879 and linking the Suffolk coastal town of its name with the Great Eastern at Halesworth, was potentially an admirable and useful concern with a reasonably heavy year-round trade, both freight and passenger, added to in summer of course by holidaymakers. Its first trouble was just that its equipment was not really up to the loads it had to handle. Like the Eskdale's, and the early Isle of Man's at least, its locomotives were actually rather small for the gauge, and even on the relatively level route could barely exceed about 20 miles an hour. Worse than any of that, the Southwold was an early victim of the disease which has laid low so much of British industry – hypertropic accountantitis – or refusal to act unless it could be assured that every move would yield the greatest profit possible. Consequently it ran the smallest number of trains it could, at the lowest practical speed, combining freight and passenger to make up a maximum load. It was therefore

The Southwold Railway trundled its passengers peacefully between its junction with the old Great Eastern Railway (later LNER) at Halesworth and the small country town of Southwold. Never noted for its speed, this little line was the butt of a local humorist Reg Carter, one of whose drawings is reproduced here. The line was the first of the casualties and all traffic ceased on 11 April 1929.
Millbrook House collection

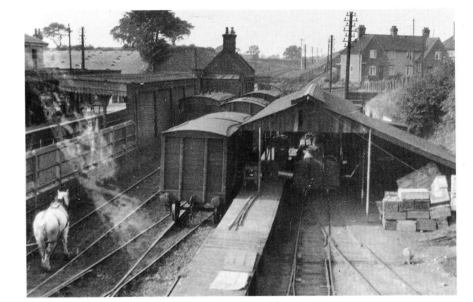

**THE SOUTHWOLD EXPRESS**  A COW ON THE LINE IS LUCKILY SEEN BY THE GUARD - IN HIS EAGERNESS TO STOP THE TRAIN HE PUTS THE BRAKES ON TOO SUDDENLY!

Halesworth, Suffolk, showing both the Great Eastern and Southwold railway stations. Note the freight interchange platform, the shunting horse and the hand-operated points.
Millbrook House collection

Southwold Railway 0–6–0 tank No 2 Halesworth (Sharp Stewart & Co Ltd, Atlas Works Manchester No 2845 of 1879) with a mixed train entering Southwold station shortly before closure.
Dr. Ian C. Allen

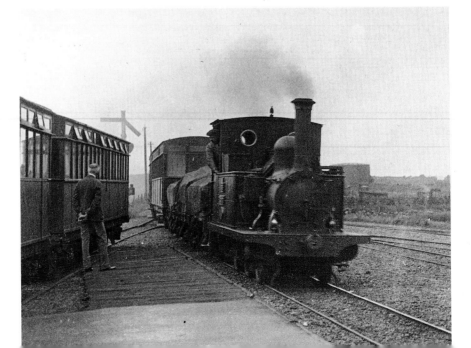

not a popular railway, and rude postcards showing its trains in embarrassing situations and its staff acting in unconventional and unhelpful ways began to be sold, and indeed can still be purchased in the area. It was all rather a pity, since it was basically a very pleasant railway running through one of the better parts of Suffolk to a town of character. It also had the only narrow-gauge swing-bridge in Britain. But finally it committed suicide; alarmed at the prospect that imminent motorbus competition might cause it to start to run at a loss, it announced one Friday in April 1929 that it was closing down the following day. Perhaps the directors expected that blackmail, which they had not tried hitherto, would prove as profitable a trade as any other; but the buses moved smoothly in to take over and nobody lifted a finger. The locomotives and stock remained where they stood, on the grassy track, until everything was swept up in a wartime scrap drive in 1942, and that was that.

Its irresponsible top management, rare if not absolutely unique in British railway history, certainly did nothing for the narrow-gauge cause in Britain, though perhaps that was not entirely a bad thing, but it also founded a number of legends which even now keep cropping up. Hardiest of them all is the one that its locomotives and its rolling stock were originally built for China, but were rejected by the Chinese as inadequate; the Southwold company then snapped them up at a cut price and foisted them on to the wretched Southwolders. One can see why this appealing story was so popular, but it was founded on nothing more than the fact that one of the promoters of the line, Richard Rapier, of the Ipswich engineering firm of Ransomes & Rapier, had indeed been one of the protagonists of the first railway in China, the 2ft 6in gauge Shanghai and Woosung, in the mid-1870s. Ransomes actually built the locomotives for the short-lived Chinese operation, but they were quite different from and smaller than the Southwold engines (built by Sharp, Stewart), while the coaches were different also. Furthermore, when the Shanghai and Woosung was closed down by the Imperial Chinese government as a disturbance of the celestial peace, its equipment was sent to Formosa and used there. So however reluctantly, one is forced to acquit the Southwold directors of something.

It can therefore be seen that at the end of the 1870s, although there were several interesting and promising concerns in Wales, the public narrow-gauge railways in England were an unimpressive bunch. This was a matter of concern to many people because it meant that where there was a fair amount of traffic moving, enough to carve up the primitive roads of the time and cause the local ratepayers much expense in repairs, but not enough to make a stan-dard-gauge railway a practical proposition, the public was being ill served. The legislature was slowly moving towards finding ways of making railway construction easier, partly by reducing its harsh original requirements laid down in the 1830s and 1840s concerning matters of bridging and fencing, but mainly by streamlining the complex and expensive legal procedures which the first railway promoters had had to negotiate. The engineering professional was

45

also finding ways of making the equipment cheaper to install and operate, in part following the example of the Festiniog Railway which had shown the way.

One man took a different and more radical tack. He put forward the argument that even a 2ft gauge line was too heavy and expensive for many situations, and that something even lighter and cheaper was needed. Sir Arthur Heywood, of Duffield, near Derby, was a man of means and at the same time an engineer. Working from first principles, he established that a gauge of 15in was the narrowest on which a vehicle would not be upset by the movements of people inside; and so, without further ado, he proceeded to construct on his own property a complete 15in gauge railway to demonstrate his ideas. He also published a book *Minimum Gauge Railways,* in which he showed how such a railway would be cheaper than road haulage, even at as low a freight movement as 6,000 tons a year, even when the additional capital expense of building and equipping the railway was taken into account. All that was needed, in other words, apart from sites where the transport need existed and could be depended on to continue, was people to provide that capital.

Unfortunately this was the difficult bit. Heywood himself expanded and enlarged his own demonstration line until it became easily the finest garden railway there has ever been. It had awesome gradients, viaducts, tunnels and yards and stations and signalboxes; it had frightful curves and a long enough straight run to open up. It had all sorts of rolling stock, including dining and sleeping cars; and the Heywood family was numerous enough to staff it and run trains all at once in every direction. It was obviously great fun, and occasionally the railway would be put on view to the public, generally for the edification of a learned society or agricultural association, and they had fun too. Only one customer ever took up Heywood's ideas and had him build a 15-in gauge railway for serious movement of freight, and that was the Duke of Westminster, whose country establishment at Eaton Hall, near Chester, was some three miles from the nearest station and needed five or six thousand tons of coal a year to keep its heating system going. But several people considered the entertainment value of railways of this kind most interesting and went away to make plans of quite a different sort. The Eaton Railway remained throughout its existence, from 1896 to 1946, a private line serving its owner solely. It had a total of 3¾miles of track and a variety of rolling stock mainly for freight, built by Heywood, but its three Heywood steam locomotives were superseded after 1918 by small diesel or petrol machines of a type developed for military service. Its main historical importance is that it was a place where other kinds of miniature railway equipment could be tried out. Although it always remained the purest expression of Heywood's ideas, it was not really a unique undertaking because it was closely paralleled by a number of industrial lines of the slightly wider 18in gauge, notably those at Crewe and Horwich railway workshops and the Royal Arsenal at Woolwich, the latter in its day a very complex and interesting system.

Three of the Lancashire &
Yorkshire Railway 0–4–0 18in
gauge 0–4–0 tanks at Horwich
Works, Robin, Wasp and Mouse.
W. Leslie Good

Jersey Railways & Tramways
Sentinel steam railcar No 2 Pioneer
at St Aubin station on 18 April
1924. This 8½ mile long 3ft 6in
gauge line was closed entirely in
1936 after a disastrous fire had
destroyed the stock.
A.W. Croughton

The other type of 15in gauge railway development may have originated with Heywood, but rapidly spread further afield, and was indeed well established in the United States by the 1890s. Its main object was not so much the provision of transport as of entertainment with miniature railways as rides for fun and profit, and its practical distinction was most obviously that the train, and the locomotive, was regarded as a model, a miniature version of current main-line practice. As such, it was not always or indeed often at all soundly engineered, while Heywood's equipment, if unorthodox and sometimes over-complex, was at least well designed and robust. However, it took Heywood over 20 years, from 1872 to 1896, to achieve even this amount of public acceptance, but in following the development of his ideas we have got rather ahead of chronological sequence.

Slowly, and following the wider acceptance of narrow-gauge railways in other parts of the world, they came to achieve some more solid progress in England and Scotland. The next new line after the Southwold was in the Channel Islands, where since the 1870s two separate short standard-gauge lines had been running east and west of the chief town of Jersey, St. Helier. One of them, the Jersey Railway, originally opened in 1870, had been linked in 1882 with a 3ft 6in gauge line serving a quarry near St Aubin, and found the narrow gauge so attractive a proposition that in 1883 it converted its original track to suit and gradually extended it, so that by 1899 it

*Jersey Railways & Tramways Bagnall 2–4–0T No 4 St Brelades at St Helier 1 September 1903.* T.J. Edgington collection

48

had reached its maximum extent – all of 8½ miles. The Jersey must have been a railway of some character and ran quite intensively; however the economics of railways on tiny islands are not very encouraging. It tried to avoid the expense of running conventional steam trains all the time by acquiring some Sentinel steam railcars; then it went into the bus business and started to run the railway in summer only. A fire in 1936 destroyed the passenger coaches and, probably with a feeling of relief, the company got out of the railway business altogether. One of its locomotives ended up shunting at a power station near Johannesburg, until the mid-1970s. Since the standard-gauge Jersey Eastern had closed earlier the railway story of the island was at an end, except for some temporary military lines built by the Germans after 1940.

Certainly the finest narrow-gauge railway in England was the next one to be built, the Lynton & Barnstaple. This 19½-mile 2ft gauge line climbed from sea level at Barnstaple Town, where it connected with the Ilfracombe branch of the London & South Western, across the hills of North Devon to a summit at Woody Bay almost 1000ft up, before descending again to its terminus at Lynton, still at a height of 700ft. Unfortunately Lynton itself was several hundred feet below the station, and Lynmouth, a little further on, at sea level again, so the L&B cannot really be said to have delivered its customers to their destination. This was its first misfortune. Its next was the fact that its engineer had seriously miscalculated the cost of carving out its right-of-way, much of which was cut into the side of the rocky hills, so the company which built and opened the railway in 1898 started and remained finan- cially hamstrung. At the Grouping in 1923 the L&B passed into the Southern Railway's hands, and the SR spent a great deal of money on improvements. Never at all meanly equipped, the L&B was by 1930 a very beautiful little railway indeed, in apple-pie order, and running through some of the loveliest parts of the West Country. But, alas, it lost money, and the SR was entirely unsentimental about that. Since it was also at the time spending a great deal on improving and electrifying many of its lines nearer London, the directors no doubt felt their public image was bright enough not to be tarnished noticeably by a minor act of ruthlessness in North

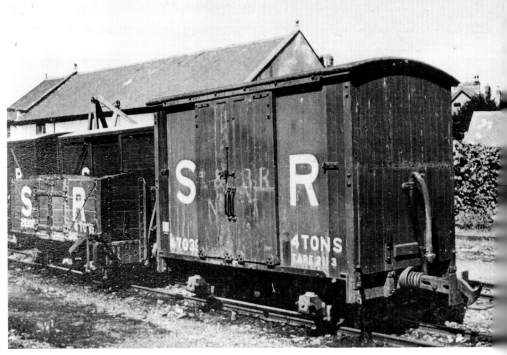

Devon. Thus in September 1935 the L&B was closed down. One of its engines ended up in Brazil, while one of its coaches, after many years as a garden hut, ended up on the Festiniog and another is now in the National Railway Museum; the rest was rapidly reduced to scrap and ashes. This was one of the first, and saddest, closures, for if the L&B had survived a little longer it would almost certainly still be running today, operated by preservationists. Its fine viaduct at Chelfham, one of the largest on any narrow-gauge line in any of the British Isles, still stands, and has been a monument for twice as long

Thor's Cave, Manifold Valley, North Stafford Railway.

*The North Stafford Railway promoted the Leek & Manifold Valley Light Railway as seen from this official postcard c. 1907.*

as it ever carried trains.

The next narrow-gauge railway to be opened, at least for public traffic, was also very fine and maintained the same high standard of design and equipment, but it was even shorter-lived. The Leek & Manifold Valley Light Railway was actually a two-part invention, and was taken over by the North Stafford shortly before it was opened in 1904. The 10 miles from Leek, junction with the North Stafford system, to Waterhouses was a standard-gauge light railway of no particular individuality, though a short branch served a very large limestone quarry which produced ballast for most railways in the Midlands, and probably explained the decision to build this section to the standard gauge. Then at Waterhouses, which was and is hardly detectable as a place, the L&MV suddenly changed gauge to 2ft 6in, and for the last 8½ miles to Hulme End wound down, and then up, a pair of the very beautiful deep gorges which cut across the limestone hills. Unfortunately the villages all tended to be on the hilltops, and at few points on the Waterhouses to Hulme End section could a passenger look out of the train window and see more than one house, usually none, and never more than three. Even Hulme End itself fell into the two-houses-and-a-pub category. It had been intended to go on to Buxton, which would have been a different matter, but alas.

On the other hand, the L&MV was very well equipped, even if not very lavishly. It only ever had two locomotives, but they were good ones, more or less identical with some on the Barsi Light

*Hulme End (for Sheen and Hartington) the far terminus of the Leek & Manifold Valley Light Railway. Note the standard-gauge sidings at the remote end of this 2ft 6in gauge line and the private owners' wagons on the transporter next to the 2–6–4 tank No 1* E.R. Calthrop. A.W. Croughton

Railway in India. It only ever had four coaches, but they were substantial bogie vehicles. It never had very many freight wagons, but it did have half a dozen transporter trucks, each capable of carrying a standard-gauge four-wheeler, and each station along the line had a short standard-gauge siding. The Manifold Valley was thus one of the few British examples of avoidance of transhipment by carrying the main-line wagon right through on the narrow-gauge, a method quite often found even now on the Continent (particularly in Austria), and indeed the best-known one, and the only example handling ordinary public freight traffic. Apart from coal, which in those days went everywhere by rail, the main business was in milk, and indeed the importance of this traffic forced the Manifold Valley to run seven days a week throughout the year, uniquely for any British narrow-gauge line. Oddly enough, in spite of this the L&MV train service was also the least frequent of any, including seasonal operation.

The transfer of wagons onto and off the transporter trucks must have been a very slick operation, too; since both standard and narrow gauge trains were mixed, carrying both freight and passenger traffic, and both were timed as a rule to arrive at Waterhouses within a few minutes of each other, and both were generally off again within 20 minutes of the first arriving. So the

*A holiday excursion on the Leek & Manifold Valley section of the LMS in the 1920s. Both locomotives and virtually all the line's stock are in use!* W.H. Whitworth

picture was one of incredible action twice a day, with hours of silence in between.

The Manifold was hardly ever discovered by tourists; the nearest it came to this was every year in Wakes Week, when all the factories and works of the Potteries closed down and the inhabitants took their annual holidays. That week the railway went mad, and every available wagon (or transporter) was fitted with seats and roofs and both engines charged up and down double-headed dragging practically everything on wheels. That week it usually earned half its total annual revenue. Unfortunately such a peaky operation only made things worse; the London Midland & Scottish therefore gave up and closed it all down in 1934, donating the right-of-way (including Swainsley Tunnel) as a bicycle path. Enthusiasts can therefore test personally how much harder one has to pedal on a 1 in 30 gradient; quite a lot, in the author's experience. But it is not steep enough to freewheel down very successfully.

The third high-grade turn-of-the-century narrow-gauge line was in Scotland, the Campbeltown & Machrihanish. In fact this grew out of an older, steam-powered, railway linking the quay at Campbeltown with a small colliery halfway across the Mull of Kintyre, which had opened in 1877. Campbeltown was very much the end of the line as far as the Clyde passenger steamers were concerned, and only just on the mainland, at the end of a very long thin peninsula, but one which kept the full force of the Atlantic breakers out of the more sheltered waters of the Clyde estuary. After some time it was felt that perhaps tourists would like to go and look at those breakers crashing onto the opposite side of the peninsula, and maybe play a round of golf while they were doing so. For very little more an objective than this, the older colliery line was rebuilt and extended in 1906 to form the six mile long, 2ft 3in gauge Campbeltown & Machrihanish. It was very well equipped, though like the Manifold Valley not very lavishly; however for some years the colliery continued to give the line extra business and the four smaller older colliery engines supplemented the two larger newer ones. The six bogie coaches were perhaps, alongside the original Welshpool & Llanfair ones built about the same time and by the same builder, the most attractive and well-designed of any narrow-

*A scene on the quay at Campbeltown on 2 August 1930. The locomotive is the Andrew Barclay 0–6–2 tank* Atlantic. H.C. Casserley

gauge passenger stock in Britain. Things were fairly quiet in winter, but in summer the tourists piled off the boats very much as predicted and came and looked at the awful ocean and played golf, and things got quite busy – until the motor car induced them to do something different. The colliery closed down about the same time, and in 1932 it all came to an end. The C&M had lasted an even shorter time than the Manifold or the Lynton & Barnstaple, and the excellence of their equipment had saved none of them.

The last new line did not aim at having excellent equipment built for it; like a number of industrial railways and even some agricultural ones (a potato railway in Lincolnshire, and a couple of grouse-moor ones in Scotland), it chose instead to use some of the vast amount of second-hand light and narrow-gauge railway equipment available very cheaply second-hand, as the military railways behind the World War 1 trenches were dismantled in the years after 1918.

In the last few years of his life, in the mid-1840s, George Stephenson had more or less retired from railway-building and had become one of the founders of the Clay Cross Company, which took over and greatly developed the coalmines, limeworks, and ironworks in the area just south of Chesterfield. The company prospered, and by 1918 sought to develop some new limestone quarries near Ashover. It therefore promoted the Ashover Light Railway, which in 1924 opened the 7½ miles of 2ft gauge from Clay Cross to Ashover to freight traffic, and the following year to passengers. Nearly half the line was in fact parallel to the Chesterfield-Derby main line, between Ashover and Stretton, though it took a different route and climbed over the hill which the latter drove under in the Clay Cross tunnel, and so some heavy locomotive work was required on this section of against-the-load gradient. From Stretton to Ashover the route was quite scenic, not unlike a more accessible Manifold Valley. Most of the equipment was second-hand ex-War Department, including the six Baldwin 4–6–0T locomotives of stark and unmitigated American aspect, though some rather more adequate coachbodies were put onto the ex-WD underframes for the passenger traffic. For a year or so this was very heavy, but buses soon reduced the flow and year-round passenger trains ceased to run in 1930 and the seasonal ones were withdrawn in 1936. Freight however continued to be handled until 1950. One reason for the short life of the line was the fact that the ex-army rail, weighing only 25 lb/yd, was not really man enough for the loads it was asked to carry and after a while the track became very rough indeed, and would have needed complete renewal long before 1950 if the output of the Ashover and Fallgate quarries had ever come up to expectations. So the Ashover did no better with second-hand equipment, and had an even shorter life than the Campbeltown & Machrihanish. It also represented the last attempt in Britain to build a fully-fledged public narrow-gauge railway for ordinary transport purposes.

There remains to be mentioned the 'minimum-gauge railways' which followed Sir Arthur Heywood's ideas. As we have seen, they could be divided into two classes—those railways which were primarily transport undertakings, for which freight movement was the main motivation, and those which were mainly for entertainment. However it proved difficult at times to maintain this distinction.

We have already described the early history of the 3ft gauge Ravenglass & Eskdale Railway in the Lake District, which had apparently succumbed after a long illness in 1913. The old 'Ratty' was indeed dead, but in this case a phoenix rose from the ashes. A group of miniature railway enthusiasts, including W. J. Bassett-Lowke, then the leading British manufacturer of model railways, arranged with the main creditor of the old bankrupt company to acquire the derelict railway, scrapped the old locomotives and stock, and regauged the track to 15in. At the same time the same people were doing the same thing at Fairbourne in North Wales. Services were resumed over the first mile from Ravenglass to Muncaster in 1915, and by 1918 the whole 6¼ miles to Boot was again working. This might seem rather a frivolous undertaking in the middle of a great war, but in fact summer holiday traffic was not yet the main business of the line; the varied transport needs of the local farming community had not been well met during the period of closure, and coal, wool, and potato loadings helped the finances where passenger revenue on its own, even with the mail contract soon added, would

*Muriel's* last days. The Duffield Bank 0–8–0 tank in use as a stationary boiler on the 15in gauge Ravenglass & Eskdale Railway in the early 1920s. A.W. Croughton

not have been enough. The worst problem was caused by the fact that Bassett-Lowke's engines, designed as models rather than for hard work, proved too flimsy and underpowered and needed to be replaced as soon as possible. The new company succeeded in obtaining most of the equipment, and all the locomotives, from Heywood's own railway at Duffield Bank after this was dismantled following his death in 1916.

During the 1920s, and not without some tribulations, the new 'Ratty's' affairs were slowly put in order, and new and even more substantial locomotives acquired. The line was one of the first in Britain to start using internal-combustion locomotives in public traffic, and in fact since the early 1920s a high proportion of its annual train mileage has always been worked by petrol or diesel machines of one sort or another. For many years until the 1950s, a mainstay of the business was granite ballast, quarried and crushed on-line by the railway company, and from 1929 to 1953 the first three miles of track from Ravenglass to Murthwaite had standard-gauge rails added to cater for this. The general non-tourist passenger, and other freight traffic gradually faded away during the 1930s and left the R&ER mainly dependent on tourists. Since 1960 it has been owned and assisted by preservation-minded people and has fought its way to its present position, as a well-run, prosperous and enterprising a concern as any that British narrow-gauge railway history can show.

Sir Robert Walker, owner of substantial estates a few miles south-east of York, had been another disciple of Heywood's and in 1912 constructed a 15in gauge garden railway in the grounds of his country mansion at Sand Hutton. He soon became fired with the idea of extending it to serve places all over his lands, linking them with the North Eastern York to Hull branch at Warthill. Work started on this scheme after the First World War, and in 1920 the line was operating from Warthill to Claxton brickworks, 2½ miles, and Sand Hutton. Until then it had been a miniature railway with one model locomotive; but at this point Walker changed tactics. He decided to purchase a quantity of Government surplus 18in gauge equipment, originating from a temporary wartime railway at Deptford, which was narrow-gauge and not miniature, and so back in the mainstream of the Heywood doctrine. The whole Sand Hutton Railway was therefore converted to 18in gauge in 1921, and reached its maximum length of seven miles in 1923. Passenger traffic was never very important, and generally trains only ran on Saturdays; tourists were not really encouraged. But freight during the 1920s amounted to a fairly substantial total, some 13,000 tons a year, often keeping two locomotives busy every day. Unfortunately Sir Robert died in 1930, and his railway did not long survive him, closing down abruptly in 1932 with the demise of the brickworks and the estate's changeover to motor transport. But for those years the Sand Hutton was a much more important and impressive operation than the Eaton railway, and a better demonstration of Heywood's principles. It was, however, the last such. The next new

narrow gauge put its weight very firmly on the other foot.

The revival and slow climb to prosperity of the 15in gauge Ravenglass & Eskdale had attracted a great deal of interest, and after 1918 a few men began to consider the possibilities of doing the same sort of thing on a much grander scale; instead of reviving a short narrow-gauge branch, to build a complete and complex main line railway in miniature, with large stations, double track, signalling, fast running, and all the trimmings. To do this it would of course be necessary to find a site where the public would use the trains, partly because having actual live passengers would be the final masterstroke of miniature realism, but also because such a railway would have to be long, too long to be contained in even the most stately and ducal of establishments. Two men in particular had such a dream, Count Louis Zborowski and J. E. P. Howey. Both were racing motorists, active in the sport at Brooklands; each was exceedingly rich, particularly Zborowski. During 1924 they tried and failed to buy the Eskdale railway; on the rebound they ordered a pair of one-third size miniature versions of Gresley's Pacifics then newly introduced on the London & North Eastern Railway, and arguably the finest express passenger locomotives then running in Britain. Certainly as 15in gauge locomotives, these were greatly superior to anything possessed by the Eskdale. Then that autumn Zborowski was killed in a motor racing accident, and Howey had to continue with the project on his own.

At the time it was a very indefinite project, since no site on which to build the railway had yet been found. But in 1926 it was found, between Hythe and New Romney, on Romney Marsh in Kent, and in 1927 Howey opened the Romney, Hythe & Dymchurch Railway, 8½ miles long, double track, and quite the longest and most lavishly-equipped miniature railway there has ever been anywhere. In 1928 he extended it a further five miles from New Romney to Dungeness,

*Pacifics No 10* Dr Syn *and No 3* Southern Maid *come to rest in Dymchurch station with the 10.35am New Romney to Hythe train during the RH&DR Spring Gala on Sunday 16 May 1993. Special events such as this 'Gala' when trains were double-headed have become a regular attraction on most tourist lines. P.J. Howard.*

to drive the point home.

The RH&DR soon became famous, and has remained so ever since. Its staple traffic has always been summer visitors; an Eskdale-type attempt to cater for year-round passenger trade with the aid of internal combustion power after 1929 was abandoned after 1945. During the war the railway was run for a period by the army, and saw quite the world's smallest armoured train; for a while afterwards, like the Eskdale, it ran a fairly heavy trade in ballast. Since recent times part of the line, between Dymchurch and New Romney, sees daily year-round service bringing children to school. But otherwise it is tourists who fill the trains, and a great number of them during the peak season. Since Howey's death in 1963 the RH&DR has seen some difficult times, but now seems likely to continue past them. Its problem, compared with the relatively prosperous Eskdale, is that it carries perhaps 50 per cent more passengers but uses roughly double the equipment, and staff, to do so, which sounds like a simple problem in productivity, and would be just that in most businesses. But railways, unlike tomato soup factories, have to fit geographical situations.

That really ends the chronological account of English (and

*In the early days of the Second World War, when invasion seemed imminent, one of the measures taken was to provide armoured trains to run on the coast railways. One of these was on the 15in gauge Romney Hythe & Dymchurch Railway in Kent; the locomotive is 4–8–2 No 5 Hercules, as modified at Ashford works. Millbrook House collection*

Scottish) narrow-gauge public railways. But it leaves much ground uncovered. For example there were a number of lines that occupied the arguable area between railways and tramways, and even if we adhere to the rule that tramways, even steam-powered, are ineligible for inclusion in this book some narrow gauge ones which called themselves tramways had many of the characteristics of a light railway, even if they ran along the highroad part of the time. There was the Alford & Sutton, in Lincolnshire, shortest-lived of all; seven miles of passenger-carrying steam-worked 2ft 6in gauge track opened in 1884 and put out of business five years later by the construction of a parallel Great Northern branch line from Willoughby to Sutton-on-Sea and Mablethorpe. There was the 3ft 6in gauge Wolverton and Stony Stratford, which ran tram engines and double-deck cars, but half its length (of 4½ miles) was certainly a rural light railway. Opened in 1886, it would have closed long before the General Strike of 1926 polished it off had not the London & North Western taken it over for the sake of its users employed at Wolverton Works. Some of these borderline concerns were even electrified, like the Midland's 3ft 6in gauge Burton & Ashby Light Railway, another service terminated by the General

Strike, or the Kinver Light Railway in Staffordshire. There was the Rye & Camber, 2½ miles of 3ft gauge in Sussex, which operated from 1895 to 1939 and called itself a tramway, but had no tram-like characteristics whatever, with its own right of way throughout, stations with platforms, locomotives that were not dressed up so as not to frighten the horses (although after the 1920s the steamers rarely appeared, supplanted by Simplex tractors). However, Bradshaw's Guide took the Rye & Camber at its own valuation, and did not include its trains.

Then we have the category of lines which started as industrial narrow gauges but which, instead of being abandoned when industry ceased to use them, were taken over by new operators and converted to passenger traffic, railway enthusiast and preservationist oriented. There are two important examples of these. The Sittingbourne & Kemsley was once a very considerable undertaking linking various of Bowater's paper mill operations in North Kent, with a large fleet of 2ft 6in gauge steam locomotives one of which was built as recently as 1953. In 1969 part of this system, linking Sittingbourne town with the main factory complex several miles away across the salt flats, was transferred to an enthusiast group, and still operates in season even though the rest of the railway has long ceased to exist and much of its equipment is scattered elsewhere. The other is at Leighton Buzzard, in Bedfordshire, where a

*One of England's lesser known gauge railways, the 2½ mile long 3ft gauge Rye & Camber Railway which ran from July 1895 to 1939. Steam rarely appeared in service after 1925, being replaced by a Simplex tractor in that year. The first section to open was from Rye to Golf Links with the extension to Camber Sands carrying traffic from July 1908, in time for the summer season. There were originally two locomotives (both 2–4–0 tanks by W.G. Bagnall) two coaches and three wagons, the locomotives being named* Camber *and* Victoria *respectively. The line was constructed under the supervision of H.F. Stephens. A.W. Croughton*

five-mile 2ft gauge line, built using ex-military equipment in the early 1920s and diesel-worked from the outset, for many years carried sand from the pits to the London & North Western, and then after the mid-1960s, only slightly truncated, went over to enthusiast operation with a fleet of small steam engines. This lightly-built and steeply-graded line was originally wholly through green fields, but in recent years its surroundings have been built up all around it and it now presents the extraordinary spectacle of occasional narrow-gauge steam trains staggering through a large housing estate. Yet another enthusiast-backed and occasionally steam-using 2ft gauge passenger line has been built from scratch, using ex-industrial locomotives and a pair of ex-Ashover coaches but the Lincolnshire Coast Light Railway is a proper public railway two miles long, near Cleethorpes.

During the 1980s several new 15in gauge railways appeared, two of them on abandoned BR roadbeds. Much the most ambitious was the Bure Valley, using the Wroxham to Aylsham (8 miles) section of the old Great Eastern Wroxham to County School branch. Laid out on a lavish scale in some respects, with large new station buildings and the only tunnel in Norfolk (replacing a level crossing), its opening in 1990 was shortly followed by the collapse of the much larger holiday-attractions company which built it, with two changes of ownership during the next three years. Dependent largely on borrowed motive power at first, it is to be hoped that its new owners will achieve the success which, perhaps because of its problems, has been slow to come. Shorter at some three miles is the Kirklees Light Railway, on the remains of the Clayton West branch near Huddersfield. Two more lines, the Cleethorpes Coast and the Heatherslaw, although of wider gauge, perhaps really belonged in the category of railways (usually miniature) in parks and zoos; well-established, quite numerous and popular attractions, which really fall outside the scope of this book.

The wide variety expands to mind-blowing point when we consider the list of industrial narrow-gauge railways. England was once very rich in these, though now very few are left (especially after the demise of the underground operations of British Coal). Gauges varied wildly; some were unique. Some were only just narrower than standard, but two railways of enormous character, each 4ft gauge and with around ten miles of route, and each long closed, were the Redruth & Chacewater in Cornwall and the Saundersfoot in Pembrokeshire. They carried tin and anthracite respectively. Many more carried coal, tin, ironstone (the South Midlands had a great number) and indeed a great variety of minerals, while a few moved timber, peat, potatoes, or even grouse and beaters. Some had proper workmen's trains; one or two, including the Snailbeach in Shropshire, had grand but never exercised powers of expansion into passenger-carrying systems, but nearly all carried passengers in the form of youngsters begging a ride on the footplate, once out of sight of the office. Quite often the office was only too pleased to arrange matters. Books could and have been written about some of these lines, or groups of them; others are still unrecorded. We cannot do more now than simply acknowledge that they existed, and give a valedictory account of one to stand for all.

By the early 1950s the Dorset firm of Pike Bros Fayle & Co, now part of the English China Clays group, had come to own all the china clay mines in Purbeck together with the two narrow-gauge tramways which took the clay down to quays on Poole Harbour. Both of them, originally separately owned, were quite ancient, and had been running for a long time before starting to use steam locomotives in the 1860s and 1870s. The Goathorn Railway, near Corfe, was 3ft 9in gauge and had a pair of odd little locally-built 0–4–0Ts; during the Second World War much of its length had been abandoned with the disappearance of coastal shipping, and all the output was transhipped onto the Swanage branch of the Southern at Goathorn Siding. This left only a mile or so of track, and when in 1947 the ancient *Thames* fell due for repairs, it was deemed cheaper to convert the whole shebang to 2ft gauge and bring in some second-hand equipment rescued from the junkyard to work it. Among the covey of job-lot lawnmowers brought in was one very strange and waterlogged shipwrecked mariner, still just able however to clank along, the 2–6–2T *Russell* from the Welsh Highland Railway, which thus ran for a few years in England before laying its bones peacefully in the Dorset chalk (from whence — but that is another story). However the Goathorn was a very poor thing compared to the nearby Furzebrook Railway, jewel of the Pike Bros Fayle & Co empire. It had also lost its last few miles to Poole Harbour during the war and now transhipped everything at Furzebrook Sidings; but a regular network of lines still ran, needing

*Snailbeach District Railway Baldwin ex WD 4–6–0 tank outside the shed at Snailbeach in 1946. Of its three steam locomotives two were ex WD Baldwins and one a 0–4–2T Kerr Stuart (802/01). The Baldwins were regauged by W. G. Bagnall from 2ft 0in nominal to 2ft 3¾in on their acquisition in 1918 from the ROD. The Baldwin numbers were 44383/16 and 44522/17 but as the works plates were removed at Bagnall it has not been possible to deduce which was which.* P.B. Whitehouse

three locomotives in steam every day as well as a diesel tractor or two, to serve several mines, quarries and open-cast china clay workings further north and west along the Purbeck hills. And the Furzebrook was an utter delight; it ran for miles through lovely unspoilt country, through the woods and across the heaths and over splendid roller-coaster ups and downs, with strange wooden-bodied wagons of curious design, with engines scattering flocks of peacocks

*On the private industrial line of Pike Bros Fayle & Co Ltd, Dorset, all locomotives carried identification with numbers in the form of Latin names;* Quintus *halts for a while in the woods near Creech Grange on 11 August 1954.* Ivo Peters

in the grounds of Creech Grange, and a new extension being built even in 1953. One remembers a school railway club visit to the line, which was always a very friendly concern and had true educational value because all the engines had names which were Latin numbers, from *Secundus* to *Septimus Primus* had long shuffled off this mortal coil, and something terrible which one did not ask questions about had happened to *Quintus*. On this trip *Quintus* was happily propelling a run of empties back to Greenspecks when the train jolted to a stop in the woods and the driver announced that the party could earn its passage because a buffer had fallen off the engine earlier that morning thereabouts, and must now be searched for. So everyone set to poking around in the boskage, and (happy day) it was one of the authors who found the missing buffer, rolled into the middle of a blackberry bush. It was not long afterwards, that the company decided that the railway would have to go, and by 1958 the tracks had been torn up and turned into lorry-roads. No doubt bits fell off the lorries from time to time; but one doubts if finding the missing fragments ever gave such pleasure to visiting schoolboys.

# CHAPTER THREE
# WALES

As we have seen, the railway and plateway system of South Wales were well started during the 18th century, in connection with the developing coal mining industry. But with only a few minor exceptions, all were converted into standard-gauge railways between 1855 and 1860, before steam locomotives were used at all widely on them, and thus in due course they became part of the national main

*Standing on one of the higher terraces of the Dinorwic quarry in 1952 is Hunslet built 0–4–0 saddle tank* Holy War. *These engines were painted red and beautifully kept but working conditions in bad Welsh winters could only be described as awful. Note the uncut slate slabs waiting to be taken to the rope worked incline and the cutting sheds. The locomotives were taken to and from these terraces for maintenance via the precipitous incline. Between working periods each locomotive rested in a small shed on its terrace.* P.B. Whitehouse

line network. The only important example of one which survived as an independent public railway was the 4ft gauge Swansea & Mumbles, five miles long, on which was introduced in 1807 the first regular passenger service of any railway in Britain. It survived, with steam and later with electric traction, until it was finally abandoned in 1960. But South Wales is not generally regarded as narrow-gauge country.

North Wales was always quite different. It had a great number and variety of narrow-gauge lines, of which the fourteen major examples and several dozen minor ones demonstrated practically the whole spectrum of railway possibilities, and a fair number still survive.

The Penrhyn Railway is commonly regarded as the first of them, and it certainly set a pattern. Opened in 1801, and just over six miles long, it connected the slate quarries above Bethesda belonging to Lord Penrhyn with the sea at Port Penrhyn, near Bangor. The quarries were already several centuries old; as a later Lord Penrhyn wrote in 1945, 'before the tracks were laid, the average cost of transport to the port was equal to the cost of production, and we read that no less than 140 men and 400 horses were engaged in carrying Penrhyn slates alone to the port. After the track was laid in 1801, a rather larger tonnage could be handled by 16 horses and 12 men and boys. This economy enabled the selling price of slates to be reduced and made it possible for the industry to cater for a wider market and the slates to be shipped to all parts of the British Isles.'

Probably in order to conform with older tracks and wagons used in the quarries themselves, the builder of the Penrhyn line, Benjamin Wyatt, fixed on a distance of 2ft (or more accurately 23in) between the rails. But he was also responsible for a unique variation, which proved durable and made North Wales the location of a very rare sub-species of railway. He disliked the plateways then common in South Wales for the sound reasons that the angled rail collected mud and dirt which made haulage difficult, and was also less strong than it should be for the weight of iron used. But he did not much like the ordinary edge railway either, for reasons he does not make so clear; instead he designed a double-flanged wheel, free to move sideways on its axle. This did have the useful advantage that track gauge could vary pretty widely without ill effect, and wagons could be brought to any part of a quarry where work was going on simply by laying rails loosely on the ground; it had the drawback that points and crossings were quite complicated. Originally Wyatt used a rail of oval section with a closely fitting concave tread in the wheel, which proved a bad idea because the wheel was almost worn out when new, and apt to bind on the rail. But when a flat tread and rail-head were substituted, a perfectly workable arrangement resulted which lasted in the area for over 150 years and even now may not be quite extinct.

Originally the Penrhyn Railway was typical of its period in another way; like a canal, it was divided into a number of level or near-level sections, with nearly all the 550ft drop from quarries to coast taken up in three self-acting inclines, very steep double-track sections on which loaded wagons descending drew empty wagons uphill by ropes and a winding-house at the summit with a powerfully-braked winding-drum. No engine or energy was needed. North Wales once held over 100 of these simple devices, forerunners of the more complex (and powered) funicular railways now much better known. But in 1876 the Penrhyn line was modernised, its original route replaced by a totally different alignment on easier and more constant gradients so that steam locomotives could be used; in this form it served the quarries through the zenith of their development in the Edwardian years and their decline subsequently, leading to closure of the railway in 1963 and redevelopment of the quarry using rubber-tyred vehicles exclusively. Throughout this century and a half the Penrhyn line remained entirely a private railway, carrying nothing except quarry traffic (though it did for many years run a daily workmen's train). It thus kept pretty much out of the public eye, and although it had a strong scenic and antique charm, evidenced for instance by the quaint lodges on each side of its exit from the yard at the Port, tourism passed it by entirely.

The next important line to be built was the rather similar Padarn, which in 1824 commenced to link the Dinorwic quarries, near Llanberis and on the opposite slope of the mountain from Llanberis, with Port Dinorwic seven miles away on the Menai Strait. Originally it was practically a copy of the Penrhyn, with the same track gauge and Wyatt's double-flanged wheel; it was also

*Slate from the Dinorwic quarry was taken down to the sea at Port Dinorwic by means of further narrow gauge tracks – the company's main line built to the unusual but logical 4ft 0in gauge enabling it to carry four 2ft gauge wagons per vehicle piggy-back fashion. The locomotive is* Amalthaea, Hunslet *(1896) built 0–6–0 tank.* P.B. Whitehouse

rebuilt for locomotives on a totally new route. In the case of the Padarn this change came earlier, in 1848, and, uncertain at that time whether steam power would prove practical on the 2ft gauge, the owners decided instead to build a new 4ft gauge steam railway from Llanberis, along the north side of the lake and so to the head of the incline leading down to Port Dinorwic. The 2ft gauge was kept at each end, and the 4ft was used exclusively for hauling loaded narrow-gauge trucks on transporter wagons (although as at Penrhyn there was also a workmen's train, using some rather quaint 4ft gauge coaches). At both quarries there were a great number of small tank locomotives employed on different levels of the workings, some of them perched inaccessibly hundreds of feet up the mountain. Each system was an amazing and little-known industrial museum and each rival undertaking was vast. But perhaps the Dinorwic, by reason of the greater age of its machinery and the antediluvian survival of its multi-gauge operation, was the more extraordinary. But it has also ceased to exist; the quarry and all its railways closed completely in 1965, although a modern 2ft gauge steam tourist railway has since been built on the old lakeside 4ft gauge trackbed near Llanberis.

Like the Penrhyn again, the Padarn throughout its existence only carried traffic to and from the quarries in the same ownership. The third significant North Wales railway was different; it was built and owned by a company incorporated by Act of Parliament, and carried all kinds of public traffic, although its staple business was slate and copper ore from the quarries and workings in the Nantlle Vale, midway between Caernarvon and Portmadoc. From the easternmost point it served in the Vale, the Pen-yr-orsedd quarry, it was 9¼ miles long, via Penygroes to a terminus on the quays at the foot of the walls of Caernarvon Castle. The Nantlle Railway was opened

*A fascinating scene at Nantlle station showing an LNWR Webb open cab 2–4–0 tank standing by the tiny turntable with a train of oil-lamped four-wheeled coaches and a very typical North Western water tank to the right. On the left in the station yard are the narrow-gauge 3ft 6in Nantlle Railway slate wagons.* National Library of Wales collection

in 1828 and also used Wyatt's double-flanged wheel, though it adopted a track gauge of 3ft 6in. From the start it took freight of all kinds for all customers, and indeed by the mid-1850s was also carrying passengers, still with horse traction.

Like the first two lines, the Nantlle was later rebuilt and modernised, but in a quite different way. Its main line was fairly easily graded, and without any rope-worked inclines; it therefore lent itself readily to conversion to a locomotive railway, although the alignment had to be changed fairly drastically to improve its curves. What actually happened, however, was that the Nantlle company was purchased by the Carnarvonshire Railway, which was constructing the Caernarvon to Afon Wen line as an ordinary standard-gauge branch; in 1866 the central section of the 3ft 6in gauge line was closed and replaced by steam trains between a point near Penygroes and a temporary station outside Caernarvon. The old horse railway remained east of Penygroes and for the last few chains onto the quays at Caernarvon, and its wagons were for some years carried between these two sections on standard-gauge transporter trucks, rather in the style of the Padarn. The passenger service was of course taken over wholly by ordinary steam trains.

The Carnarvonshire Railway was very soon absorbed by the London & North Western, which during the 1870s converted the quayside lines in Caernarvon, and also the short Penygroes to Nantlle section, to standard gauge. But the remaining two miles or so from the new Nantlle terminus to the Pen-yr-orsedd and other quarries was for various reasons never altered, and it remained a strange 3ft 6in gauge horse tramway, using double-flanged wheels, for almost another 100 years, not closing in fact until 1963. By then it had been perhaps the oddest outpost of successively the London & North Western and London Midland & Scottish Railway Companies and British Railways (London Midland Region), which must have been mightily embarrassed by it. In fact, since the Pen-yr-orsedd quarry is one of the few in North Wales still producing slate, it might conceivably still be operating except for the remorseless British Railways policy of closing down its general freight business followed throughout the 1950s and 1960s; the Nantlle fragment had to go in 1963 because the standard-gauge line it connected with was closing down as well. Although always legally a public railway, the Nantlle had by modern times, except on the converted section, more or less reverted to serving a single user; in that sense it ended on a similar footing to the Padarn and Penrhyn lines, and like them remained very little known to the general public.

The fourth major North Wales railway turned out to be utterly different in every possible way, though at its inception it was intended to be very much the same as the others. The story goes that during 1830 Samuel Holland, proprietor of one of the larger slate quarries at Blaenau Ffestiniog, was travelling to Caernarvon when at the inn at Penygroes he met one Henry Archer, a young man of means who was looking for an interesting business that would give him something to do. He was thinking of leasing the Nantlle Railway (which for most of its independent existence was actually operated by a lessee). Holland warned him not to have anything to do with it; a very much better railway project would be to build a new line from Blaenau Ffestiniog to Portmadoc. This was perhaps the genesis of the Festiniog Railway Company, which was incorporated by Act of Parliament in 1832 and opened its 13½ mile line for business four years later. Like the Nantlle, it was a public railway, carrying traffic for all comers, and after some years (certainly by 1850) it was carrying passengers as well. But it adopted the 2ft (or in this case 1ft 11½ in) gauge of the Penrhyn and Padarn lines, and its engineering was original. As a temporary measure, it had to use a pair of rope-worked inclines, one driven by a waterwheel, to get over a spur of the hills, but in 1840 it completed a tunnel nearly half a mile long through that spur and achieved the form of working originally intended, with horses drawing empty and part-loaded (with general freight) wagons up the long continuous gradient, and trains loaded with slate returning downhill powered by gravity, the horses riding in comfort in special 'dandy-carts' attached to the back of each train. This putting of the cart before the horse was not only one of the noted sights of the district, but a useful saving; none of the engineers of the earlier lines had thought of anything as clever as that, and indeed the Nantlle had a section of gradient rising against the prevailing loads. Finally, the Festiniog spurned the double-flanged wheel, since the gravity run would hardly be possible if it were used, even though it was already and for over a century remained in use on the internal tracks of

*A doubleheader on the Nantlle Railway in 1958; two horses and ten double-flanged wagons on the last section of this early 3ft 6in gauge railway, which remained a British Railways operation until 1963!*
James I.C. Boyd

An official photograph taken for the Gloucester Carriage & Wagon Co Ltd showing a new coach built for the Festiniog Railway. The date shown on the board is 1879. Note the wharf in the background. Millbrook House collection

most of the Blaenau quarries, and instead chose the greatly superior edge rail and single flanged wheel.

Apart from being longer and better engineered than any of its predecessors, the Festiniog was also a much bolder conception. For most of its length in the descent from Blaenau, some 700ft above sea level, the line was carried high up along the hillsides, round many violent curves and on a constant alternation of cuttings and embankments in or on the rock. Scenically it was very fine, though arguably Padarn and Penrhyn were both even finer; but as a feat of engineering it stood quite apart. For the last mile into Portmadoc Harbour it ran across the Traeth Mawr, the long embankment by which between 1808 and 1811 William Maddocks had reclaimed the salt marshes of the Glaslyn estuary.

Blaenau Festiniog GWR station in 1935. The train is for Portmadoc Harbour and the locomotive probably double Fairlie No 3 Taliesin. This was the exchange station with the GWR line to Bala Junction. The other connecting station was the next stop westbound and was adjacent to the LMS (ex LNWR) Conway Valley branch terminus worked at that time by ex LNWR 0-6-0 18 in goods locomotives of Victorian vintage. H.F. Wheeller

*One of the Falcon (1878) 0–4–2 saddle tanks with a train at Corris station in the early years of the railway. Note the stovepipe chimney (most photographs of the engines show the more normal flared top) and the proliferation of station staff. On the left are two wagons of uncut slate. Two of the ex Corris engines were sold to the Talyllyn Railway in 1951 (at £25 each plus £25 carriage) by the Swindon authorities. These were Nos 3 and 4 (Falcon 323/78 and Kerr Stuart 4074/21), both 0–4–2 saddle tanks.* National Library of Wales

Throughout the 19th century the Festiniog prospered very greatly, and as we have already seen never more so than after it had introduced steam traction in 1863, which it proved able to use successfully, despite much contrary advice, without either widening the gauge or easing many of its curves, although experience soon showed the need for more substantial track than it had used in the days of horse power. Its prosperity reinforced its obvious technical success and was itself a main reason for the degree of world interest it aroused. In later years it fell on hard times, partly because of the decline in the slate trade after 1914 but also a series of ill-judged commercial adventures and a lot of plain bad management; it lay closed and derelict from 1946 to 1954, when new ownership set it on a new course, handling seasonal passenger traffic and making much of its scenic and historical interest, and ultimately succeeded in reopening the whole route to Blaenau in 1982, considerably deviated once more over the same spur of the mountains that had been a problem in 1836. It is now again, like it was 100 years ago, undeniably the premier narrow-gauge railway in Britain.

The next two important lines were rather remote from Snowdonia, but both still concerned with slate, in particular with the seams of slate running across southern Merioneth from Dinas Mawddwy to Towyn. Never worked as successfully as the greater quarries of Caernarvonshire, all the same the slate produced in this area was of some commercial importance during the years of the trade. The first narrow-gauge railway in the district was the Corris, Machynlleth and River Dovey Tramroad, whose ten miles of 2ft 3in gauge horse-powered line linking the various quarries in the Corris and Aberllefenni areas with navigable water at Derwenlas, on the River Dovey 2½ miles west of Machynlleth, was opened in 1859. This was a much humbler enterprise than the Festiniog, built very economically; almost its only noticeable piece of civil engineering was a timber trestle (later replaced by a girder bridge) across the Dovey. For most of its length it followed a twisting and steeply-graded course, hemmed in between the road and the river climbing the narrow valley of the Dulas, which only opened out sufficiently to allow a few hundred yards of straight track at a time for the last couple of miles above Corris village.

Almost at once the Machynlleth-Derwenlas section was super-seded by the standard gauge of the Cambrian Railways main line to Aberystwyth, which opened in 1863, though both lines did operate side-by-side for a number of years. It was some time before the Corris Railway Company (as it had by then become) ventured to do anything to upgrade its property into a passenger-carrying steam railway, and indeed it was not until 1878, the year in which the railway oddly enough passed into the hands of the company which owned the trams in Bristol, that three small tank engines were set to work hauling freight, while horses continued to work the passenger service. This echo of early days on the Stockton & Darlington lasted for a few years until the track had been relaid with steel rail and the engines improved, when steam passenger trains began to run to Corris in 1883 and Aberllefenni in 1887.

*A turn of the century photograph of a Talyllyn Railway train at Abergynolwyn station. The locomotive is the line's 0–4–2 saddle tank No 1* Talyllyn *built in 1864 by Fletcher Jennings, Whitehaven.*
Millbrook House collection

An inter-war photograph of the 2ft 3in gauge Talyllyn Railway taken at Dolgoch. The company possessed but two locomotives both built by the Whitehaven firm of Fletcher Jennings. They were quite different, No 1 being an 0–4–2 saddle tank named Talyllyn (1864) while No 2 Dolgoch (1866) shown here, was an 0–4–0 tank with a long wheel-base. No 2 was named Pretoria for a short period during the Boer War.
Millbrook House collection

Wharf station Towyn, the terminus and rail exchange point of the Talyllyn Railway. Note the complete absence of any platform, also the weighbridge and stacked cut slate. This scene remained virtually unchanged (bar slow degeneration) from 1865 to 1951.
Talyllyn Railway Company

For nearly 50 years after that the Corris ran a surprisingly brisk and efficient little operation, branching out into running motor buses which became rather a thorn in the flesh of the Great Western Railway, which had by then taken over the Cambrian. No doubt the backing of the capitalists of Bristol was an advantage. But it was all too good to last; in 1931, as part of a settlement between the Bristol Tramways and the GWR the Corris was handed over to the capitalists of Paddington, who instantly took off the passenger trains. From then until closure in 1948 the Corris ran gently downhill all the way, though its traffic never dwindled to vanishing point and the end was quite sudden, precipitated by flood damage to the Dovey Bridge. Indeed, the $2\frac{1}{2}$ miles from Aberllefenni to the ultimate terminus of the line at Ratgoed survived a little longer, not closing until 1952. This section had never been improved and still served a remote and roadless valley with horse traction; it was thus another curiosity of the first few years of British Railways, though by then the horse had very little left to do.

The nearby Talyllyn Railway, which served the Bryneglwys quarries on the opposite side of the same range of mountains, was a much grander affair altogether when it opened in 1865. It had the same gauge (2ft 3in) as the Corris, but was from the start planned as a steam-worked passenger-carrying railway, and built very substantially, with easy curves and gradients. It was technically a public railway, although owned wholly by the quarry company. It connected with the standard gauge Cambrian Coast line, which opened simultaneously, at Towyn, and passenger trains ran as far as Abergynolwyn ($6\frac{1}{2}$ miles). Locomotives ran a further $\frac{3}{4}$-mile, along a scenic ledge rather reminiscent of the Festiniog, to the foot of a self-acting incline, from whence a couple of miles of horse tramway

*Glynceiriog station, Glyn Valley Tramway on 31 May 1932. Note the neat platform and mixed train of four wheeled stock. The engine about to run round the train is the Beyer Peacock 0–4–2 tank (2970/88)* Dennis.
H.C. Casserley

and two more inclines took the track up into the workings at Bryneglwys.

Built and equipped originally on as lavish a scale as the Penrhyn, the Talyllyn never prospered. Bryneglwys was also developed on a grand scale, and produced very high-grade and rather expensive slate, but never achieved any real profitability. Although some slate continued to be produced until 1948, both enterprises were in decline by 1900 and were kept going from 1911 until he died in 1950 only by the doggedness and sense of duty of their owner, Sir Henry Haydn Jones. By then the railway was a byword for mechanical collapse and decrepitude; the chances of some sort of derailment on any journey were better than one in ten. The revival and reconstruction of the line from 1951, when it was taken over by the Talyllyn Railway Preservation Society as the first of the enthusiast-operated railways in Britain (and the world) is a well-recorded story.

The next railway to be built, the Glyn Valley, was really the last of the old group, dependent on and growing out of the slate trade, and actually represented something of a reversion to an earlier pattern. While the Talyllyn from the outset was intended as a public steam passenger-carrying railway, the Glyn Valley was opened in 1873 as a purely horse-worked roadside tramway, 8¾ miles long, from the Shropshire Union Canal at Gledrid Wharf, near Chirk, past Glynceiriog to the slate and granite workings around Pandy. The canal remained in active commercial use at this date because it belonged to the LNWR but served territory occupied by the Great Western. The Glyn Valley's gauge was the rather odd one of 2ft 4½in, which seems never to have been explained very satisfactorily. Once again passengers were soon being carried; but partly because of some difficulties of right of way and gradient it was not until 1891 that a connection was put in with the GWR at Chirk station and a new wharf built on the canal, and locomotives took over the traffic. The Glyn Valley ran through much easier country and had even less in the way of engineering and technical difficulty than the Corris, except for the fact that the steep climb up to Chirk was against the load, which presented an expensive problem in haulage that all the other Welsh narrow-gauge railways managed to avoid. Because the tracks ran literally at the side of the road, the GVT was also unique in originally having to use tram engines, with their wheels and motion cased in. According to no less an authority than an Act of Parliament, steam engines thus disguised presented a less frightening appearance to horses. It is just as well that locomotive valve gears were generally between the frames during this period; if the wisdom of our legislators is to be trusted, the contemplation of outside Walschaerts valve gear would have driven any 19th-century horse quite crazy, though more sophisticated 20th-century ones are evidently better able to stand this kind of nervous wear and tear. Or maybe the relevant clause in the Tramways Act was settled about three o'clock in the morning, when the legislative minds were less acute than usual.

Be that as it may, the Glyn Valley achieved a modest prosperity for a number of years, though since much of its traffic after 1920 consisted of crushed stone for road improvements; every loaded wagon it carried was really another nail in its coffin. Its passenger service ceased in 1933, with total abandonment two years later. Particularly with its roadside location, it had much more in common with many Irish narrow-gauge lines than any other in Wales or most in England.

The next new line, though it reverted to the narrower 1ft 11½in gauge, was a railway through and through, with its independent trackbed throughout and, to start with at any rate, an extremely ambitious set of intentions. The North Wales Narrow Gauge Railway was intended to run from Caernarvon via Beddgelert to Portmadoc (where it would link with the Festiniog), with a short branch from Tryfan Junction to Bryngwyn which would, by means of an incline, serve the quarries on the north side of the Nantlle Vale and so pinch some customers from the London & North Western. From Beddgelert a second and very long line would climb over the shoulder of Snowdon via Capel Curig to Bettws-y-Coed, and then persevere even further across a long stretch of open and desolate country, with few mineral workings, eventually to reach Corwen, only some 20 miles from the English border. These lines, had they been built, would have totalled some 60 miles; needless to say most never were. With great difficulty, the NWNGR managed to raise funds to complete between 1877 and 1881 the 9¼ miles from Dinas Junction, three miles south of Caernarvon on the LNWR's old Nantlle section, to Rhyd-Ddu, plus the three-mile Bryngwyn branch. But there it got stuck. It was a well-built little undertaking with some good equipment, not surprisingly since some of the leading lights of the Festiniog were involved with it. But although the short Bryngwyn line was quite busy before 1914, the main line never achieved what had been hoped, despite the stroke of renaming Rhyd-Ddu station South Snowdon in a surprisingly successful move to attract visitors to the mountain. Admittedly the summit was only three miles away, but a good fraction of the distance was vertical. Things were not helped by the failure to reach the main traffic objective of Caernarvon. Very soon bankrupt, the NWNG staggered on; its passenger trains ceased to run in 1916, and in the natural course of things it would have died a few years later.

But the natural course of things was for once not followed. More determined efforts were made to keep the NWNG alive, and complete at least part of its original scheme, than almost any other struggling railway in Britain. In 1906 another company, the Portmadoc, Beddgelert & South Snowdon, set about linking the NWNG and the FR with an electric railway with a ruling gradient of 1 in 22; it achieved quite a lot of part-finished formation and laid about four miles of track.

It was responsible for the ½-mile tunnel in the Aberglaslyn Pass and some dead-end embankments around Beddgelert which remain to fox curious tourists. Finally, after 1918, almost every local authority in the area mortgaged itself to the back teeth in a final desperate effort to complete the line, with success at last; the moribund NWNG was rebuilt and the splendid new Welsh Highland Railway, 21 miles long, from Dinas via Beddgelert to Portmadoc opened in 1923. It was the longest narrow-gauge line in England and Wales, and by means of some bold engineering the gradient above Beddgelert was cut from 1 in 22 to a still very taxing but less impossible 1 in 40.

It all turned out to be a most appalling disappointment. The money raised had only just been enough to lay the track and erect some tin shanty stations; not one single new locomotive or item of rolling stock could be afforded, although one ex-War Department 4–6–0T was added to the stock of ex-NWNG engines, to replace one, needless to say the best, which had had to be sold during the war to help pay the wages. The Railway Inspectorate was alarmed about many defects, including the lack of signalling and such things as station floors in a state of collapse. The revived idea of extending to Caernarvon had to be dropped once more, and the WHR remained stuck at Dinas. There had to be a level crossing with the GWR at Portmadoc, with a GWR signalbox and signalman for which the WHR had to pay; in some years it could not afford to do so, and passengers were made to get out and walk across the GWR to a Festiniog train waiting on the other side. The Welsh Highland

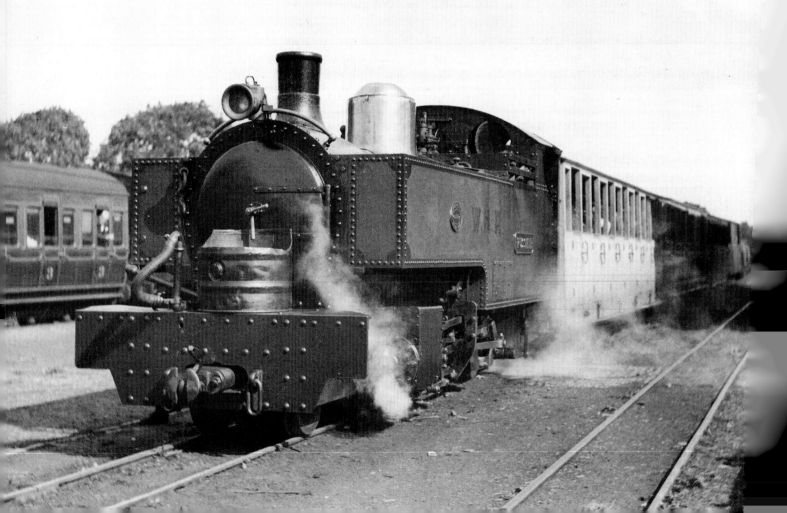

company was bankrupt within a few months of opening, and things went quickly from bad to worse; throughout one season in the 1930s one locomotive was out of action since one of its driving wheels was impounded against payment of their account by the Hunslet Engine Company in Leeds, while another was moribund, and only one engine was available to work the whole peak-season traffic.

The independent Welsh Highland gave up the struggle soon after, at the end of 1933. Closure was postponed a little longer, since the Festiniog leased the railway and from 1934 to 1936 inclusive trying very hard to make a go of it, putting on a reasonably good and dependable service; all that was achieved was to strain the Festiniog's own finances dangerously. A lot of money had to be spent renovating the four miles of track laid by the PBSS after 1906 which had been left unaltered in 1923. The whole thing finally ground to a halt at the end of the 1936 season, though due to the legal complications resulting from the fact that the railway was bankrupt anyhow, it took the overriding authority of the wartime scrap drive to get the track lifted in 1941, while the Welsh Highland company still exists on paper.

So it was all, in the end, a very sad story, and it took a long time for the hard feelings engendered to die down, while the ratepayers of the area remained saddled with a permanent load of debt (still, inflation has since made a nonsense out of that). But as always with the most lost causes, the Welsh Highland has a stronger air of doomed and desperate romance about it than any other narrow-gauge line in the principality, and more ghosts haunt its waterlogged cuttings and rusting steel bridges than most other abandoned sites. The very beauty and hopelessness of the location, and the short life of the completed railway add to this appeal.

It must be recorded that not only was the ghost of the old Welsh Highland still walking as the second edition of this book was being prepared, but showing distinct signs of preparing to come back to life. One group of preservationists has rebuilt and restored the last surviving ex-WHR locomotive, imported several more, and occupies a short section of ex-Cambrian Railways land at Portmadoc; while another and better-funded organisation backed by the Festiniog Railway is proposing actually to rebuild the whole line, taking the opportunity afforded by the closure of the standard gauge railways in the area of starting at the originally intended and never achieved destination of Caernarvon. It is perhaps in keeping with the character of the old NWNGR that the earliest manifestations of returning life have been expensive legal confrontations and complexities, but the tempting image of a Garratt-hauled train storming up the whiplash curves above Beddgelert and snaking across the slopes of Snowdon above Quellyn Lake conjures up more than druidical phantoms at last. Fingers crossed!

This is perhaps a good moment to break off from our chronological account of the different Welsh narrow-gauge systems by going back in time to have a look at the various other lines that connected

Opposite:
*Welsh Highland Railway No 12 Russell is seen in immaculate condition at Dinas Junction in 1937. Built in 1909 by Hunslet of Leeds, the locomotive first saw service with the North Wales Narrow Gauge Railway, the cab and boiler fittings being cut down later when the WHR took over and the service extended to Portmadoc through the Aberglaslyn Pass. Following closure of the line the engine was overhauled at the Brymbo Steel Works before seeing service on the ironstone line at Hooknorton near Banbury from 1942 to 1948 when it was acquired by B. Fayle & Co who used it on their lines in Dorset. After closure of this system, a further move was made to the Narrow Gauge Railway Museum at Towyn where it resided from 1955 to 1965. Restoration was then undertaken on different sites until Russell was returned to Wales in 1977 to work from a site near Portmadoc BR station being developed by a new Welsh Highland Railway as a base for a tourist line.*
Millbrook House collection

with the Festiniog. There were three altogether. The first, the Croesor Tramway, an 8-mile line linking Portmadoc Harbour with the slate workings in the Croesor Valley, which were on the opposite side of the mountain from the main workings around Blaenau Festiniog, commenced operations in 1864. It was a horse-worked affair at all times, reverting to primeval engineering in avoiding all possible earthworks and using a series of inclines to reach its objectives; however in 1923 some four miles at the seaward end were rebuilt and taken over to form the Welsh Highland's entry into Portmadoc. Slate production in the Croesor Valley ceased in 1930, but in hopes of resurrection the track was kept in even after the rest of the WHR was dismantled in 1941, and only removed during the 1950s. The second FR connection, the Gorseddau, was a 13-mile line running north of Portmadoc to some remote quarries not far (as the crow might fly) from the Nantlle Vale, part of which used the route of an earlier 3ft gauge tramway. The Gorseddau was actually opened in 1875 as a locomotive-worked line, but it was premature, having been built before the quarries it served were properly proven. They turned out to be duds. Much of the Gorseddau was closed down the same year it opened; the rest survived on a thin dribble of traffic until 1892. No official passenger service ever ran, though if things had gone differently it might have; certainly people were carried unofficially.

The most important FR feeder line was the Festiniog & Blaenau, a 3½-mile locomotive-worked freight and passenger railway of a substantial class, opened in 1868. It connected with the FR at Dolgarregddu Junction, in Blaenau Ffestiniog, and ran on a twisting hillside course through quite a populous area, serving numerous quarries, to the much older town of Ffestiniog, from which Blaenau had taken part of its name. It was owned by an independent company, however, and had a fairly short life as a 2ft gauge line; in 1883 it was purchased by the Great Western and converted to standard gauge to form the final section of its branch from Bala, completed the same year. The Bala to Blaenau was a remote and rather lovely line, remarkable among other things for its appalling curves at the Blaenau end, little modified from the original narrow-gauge alignment. Oddly enough, although the rest of the line was closed in 1961, the old F&B section remains in existence and still sees an occasional diesel-hauled train, going to the Trawsfynydd Nuclear Power Station to remove spent fuel. The F&B as a standard-gauge line was remarkable for another thing as well. Some of the quarries it served kept their own 2ft gauge connections and slate wagons, and continued to send their slate away in these wagons, either down the Festiniog Railway to the sea or simply to Blaenau for transfer to the London & North Western. The latter Company had its own station there, and until 1961 the two standard-gauge stations in the town were not linked except by the Festiniog. In order to accommodate this traffic, the Great Western therefore had to provide some transporter trucks to ferry the narrow-gauge wagons along this short length, and they remained in

The Fairbourne Miniature Railway at Fairbourne station in 1938. Note the GWR (ex Cambrian) line in the background with the clerestory roofed camping coach in the siding adjacent to the single platform halt-type station. The locomotive (at that time the line's only motive power) is the Bassett-Lowke built 4–4–2 No 3 Count Louis named after the famous racing driver who became a progenitor of the Romney, Hythe & Dymchurch Railway in Kent. The Railway was then (as now) a popular route with visitors wishing to connect with the ferry to Barmouth across the Mawddach estuary at Penrhyn Point.
P.B. Whitehouse

existence in a back siding at Blaenau (GW) almost until 1961.

From the 1880s, following the construction of the North Wales Narrow Gauge Railway itself, the growing importance of the summer visitor, or tourist traffic, as a source of revenue heralded the start of what might be termed the 'modern' era. The new accessibility of the Welsh coast and mountains, coupled with the greater prosperity of the times, meant that for the first time pleasure and leisure travel began to be worth thinking about. Railway promoters were, however, very slow to venture into this new area and in the 1880s and 1890s the running was made by horse-drawn tramways, which often developed from local mineral lines into more elaborate passenger-carrying affairs. Since they were all in general on the far side of the railway/tramway boundary, there is not the space here to delve too deeply; they were all concerns of interest and nevertheless worth noticing briefly. There were four important examples.

Horse-drawn to the end (1927), the Pwllheli & Llanbedrog Tramway was a 3½ mile long 3ft gauge concern built to gain access to his estates by Solomon Andrews of Cardiff in 1897. This photograph was taken shortly after opening c. 1901.
Mrs A. Whitehouse

Simplest perhaps was the Pwllheli & Llanbedrog, a 3 ½ mile 3ft gauge concern completed for passengers in 1897, and which was a colourful small show until storm damage caused its closure in 1927. It was built by Solomon Andrews, a developer from Cardiff who put up a lot of speculative housing on the Welsh coast at the time, and who wanted the trams to give access to his estates, which tended to be in pleasant spots not near any existing town or railway station. He had earlier, in 1890, built a similar but smaller horse tram at Fairbourne, on the opposite side of the Mawddach estuary from Barmouth; a two mile 2ft gauge affair among the sand dunes (with another, shorter-lived, close by). It proposed to take people to Barmouth by using the rowing-boat ferry from Penrhyn Point, competing with the possibility of walking, or riding, across the Cambrian Railway's bridge. Not surprisingly the Fairbourne horse tram was collapsing gently by 1916 when it was suddenly purchased by Narrow Gauge Railways Ltd, a company concerned with 15in gauge miniature railways, and over a period rebuilt it as a steam-operated seasonal line in that gauge. In spite of various ups and downs over the years it still survives, carrying very much the kind of traffic originally intended.

The two other coastal passenger tramways were both at Llandudno, and date from the same period. The Great Orme Railway, an odd half-breed, something between a tram and a funicular, still operates (thanks to Llandudno Council). Its two miles of 3ft 6in gauge is divided into two sections, with a winding-house in the middle powering both. This has been electrified in recent years, but still in the 1950s had a pair of smoking steam engines hauling the ropes. The lower, steeper, section climbs among the narrow back lanes of the town; the upper end is more open. The Llandudno & Colwyn Bay had no pretensions to being anything but an electric tram and so really ought not to be in this book; but it was such a fine one it seems a pity to leave it out. Anyhow, on the climb over the Little Orme it had a long stretch of its own right-of-way, so perhaps it will qualify. Its eight miles of 3ft 6in route were getting a bit dilapidated, and the trams themselves, mainly second-hand, were quite elderly; but for it to close in 1956, when its rarity value was already obvious, was appalling. The operating company thought it could continue independently, with some hand-me-down buses, competing with Crosville; they soon learned better.

It is perhaps significant that the Snowdon Mountain Railway started by calling itself the Snowdon Mountain Tramroad; the name was not altered until 1928. In the mid-1890s electric trams were the latest fun thing, and although the mountaineering and conservationist fraternity had long resisted the idea of having a rack railway up the highest mountain in England and Wales, offended by the idea of snorting steam engines taking up hordes of banana-peel-scattering lower-class trippers without effort, somehow a nice clean smokeless tram gliding silently uphill, powered by highly ecological hydro-electricity, was less upsetting. However there were some slight snags about dams and water supplies, so the steam engines

pushed their way in all the same and are still there, complete with every predicted morsel of banana and worse.

The Snowdon line did not get off to a very good start. It adopted a gauge which had already become the principal standard for Swiss mountain lines, 800mm, and indeed purchased its locomotives, coaches, and all other equipment straight out of the catalogue of the Schweizerische Lokomotiv und Maschinenfabrik company of Winterthur. But the SMR did not pay much attention to the fine print of the instruction book. The line was lightly built, with constantly varying gradients, and the track very roughly laid and poorly ballasted. It reached the Summit in January 1896; works and trial trips on the ill-made road caused a lot of wear and the opening day that April passed into legend when engine No 1, with the first public train on its way down, successively de-racked, derailed, and leapt over a precipice. There was a fuss. Since the line had been built without an Act of Parliament and on private land, the Railway Inspectorate could not investigate unless invited; but they were, and over the next 12 months, during which the line remained closed, matters were sorted out and put to rights. The fundamental flaw had been the bad track; unfortunately this fact was obscured by the Inspectorate, for once not at its usual high form, deciding that Swiss engineering was inadequate and de-racking could be prevented by having some angle-iron guidebars bolted each side of the rack rail, gripped by hooks on the engine. The SLM pointed out that this arrangement would not in fact prevent de-racking, which could only be avoided by keeping the track in accurate line and level, with changes of gradient made gradual, not acute. The Snowdon remains the only rack railway in the world to use these ineffective guidebars.

However, from 1897 on the Snowdon Railway has operated successfully, and each year still carries large numbers of happy visitors to the top. It is, of course, purely a tourist railway; the only freight it carries are supplies for the cafeteria and shops at the

*For the last 100 years the Snowdon Mountain Railway has always restricted its trains to a single coach, though its locomotives are well able to handle two, as seen in this 1896 photograph of a pre-opening test run on the viaduct at Waterfall. The locomotive is No 1* Ladas, *which met a violent end on the railway's first opening day; the coaches carry the owing company's full name – Snowdon Tramroad & Hotels Company Limited.*
National Railway Museum

Summit, although during the Second World War the line was taken over by the government and although some public trains continued to run was used for military purposes, including radar experiments. The mountain top made a pretty good permanent stone aeroplane for these.

The same year as the Snowdon had its second and more successful opening, 1897, saw the completion of the Hafan & Talybont, a seven-mile 2ft 3in gauge tramway which ran from Llandre station, on the Cambrian between Machynlleth and Aberystwyth, via Talybont to some granite quarries on Hafan mountain. It was another Gorseddau. It served a remote and deserted area, and in spite of fierce grades (1 in 30 and steeper) ultimately needed a great incline as well to reach its destination. It had a large and curious vertical-boiler engine, more powerful and sophisticated than the numerous little de Wintons which almost every quarry in Caernarvonshire (and the Gorseddau) operated, but which was an abject failure; most work was done by a little 2-4-0T. It put on a passenger service for a few months. But the granite was no good. The whole enterprise collapsed in 1898, and that was that; and, as it happened, the H&T was the last Welsh narrow gauge built for mineral traffic, so it marked the end of the line of development which had started with the Penrhyn in 1801.

The next new line, the Vale of Rheidol, admittedly carried minerals in the form of lead and copper ore, and maybe people hoped this business was going to amount to something, but in fact tourist traffic was always seen as the major justification for the railway and as things turned out the Rheidol proved almost as passenger-oriented a concern as the Snowdon. The 11¼ miles of 1ft 11½in gauge, from Aberystwyth to Devil's Bridge, was opened to freight and passenger traffic in 1902. The freight side never amounted to very much, although a short branch was laid in to Aberystwyth harbour to accommodate any ore being sent away by sea. There was a fair number of small mines in the Rheidol Valley, some conveniently close to the track, enabling trains to be stopped at the tunnel mouth so that wagons could be loaded as they waited, plus a rather larger one on the other side of the valley which brought its produce across on an awe-inspiring cableway. This more important mine was actually given a short siding by the VoR company so that it could load wagons at leisure. Other mines sent their tonnage by horse and cart to Devil's Bridge station. It was all pretty small beer. But passenger business, particularly in summer, was something else. Aberystwyth was a seaside resort town of some size, and the ride to Devil's Bridge, climbing high above the narrow Rheidol valley on a long 1 in 50 grade, was arguably more spectacular than anything any of the other Welsh narrow-gauges could offer, even the Festiniog. In addition, the Rheidol had the largest and most powerful, if also arguably the ugliest, locomotives of any Welsh narrow-gauge line; only the Fairlies of the Festiniog could compare with them. To work the light winter trains they also purchased and converted the little 2–4–0 tank from the Hafan and Talybont.

84

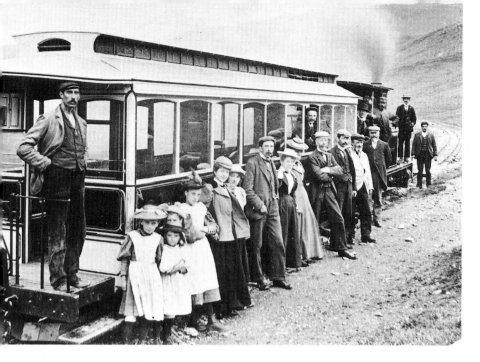

The Rheidol did not survive for long as an independent company; in 1913 it was acquired by the Cambrian, and so in due course it passed to the Great Western and to British Railways. At times BR gave the impression of being as embarrassed by its last remaining steam trains on the VoR, as it might have been earlier by its horse-drawn freight at Nantlle and at Ratgoed. But although it lost money on the line, political pressures forced it to keep it running for a long time, until at last, and in a very run-down state, it was sold to new owners in 1988. The Cambrian had also given the impression of regarding the line as a bit of a nuisance; it rapidly painted everything a poisonous dark green and paid it no further attention. The Great Western, on the other hand, did nobly by the railway, perhaps because the Chairman took a personal interest. It relaid most of the track with new rail, it built new locomotives at once, at a time when Swindon was overloaded with other work and cannot have relished such diversion of effort, and it provided new coaches later. And it kept things safely mothballed through the war, so that services could be resumed quickly in 1945, as one of the first things back to normal. One cannot blame the GWR for taking off

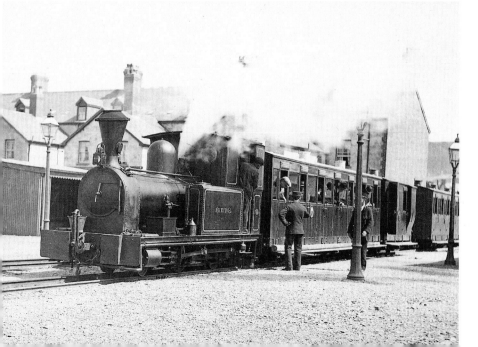

Opposite:
*Timetable, North Wales Narrow Gauge Railways dated 25 June 1892 and issued at Dinas Station.*
P.B. Whitehouse collection

*The Snowdon Railway is Britain's only steam operated rack railway. Built to the Abt system it was opened in 1896 and is to the continental gauge of 800mm (2ft 7¹/₂in). The photograph shows No 6* Padarn *blasting up the final 1 in 5 climb into Summit Station. Lake Lanberis is visible on the middle left.*
P.J. Howard

the freight service, and the winter passenger trains, in 1931; these did a vanishingly small business.

The last new narrow-gauge line to be built in Wales, the Welshpool & Llanfair, was an oddity, and had nothing in common with any of the others. In the first place, it never had any pretensions of serving any mines or quarries; it did use the formation of an old tramroad through Welshpool town between the canal and the Stondart granite quarry, but this had been abandoned long before the W&L was thought of. Its nine miles of 2ft 6in gauge merely linked a market town on the Cambrian mail line with a large village Llanfair Caereinion, which had never had any rail connection, and its traffic was purely local and agricultural. It had violent gradients, climbing for several miles out of Welshpool on a ruling 1 in 29 and then descending into the Banwy valley nearly as steeply. Two engines were always enough to handle its traffic, and they were puny machines whose rated load up the hill was seven four-wheeled wagons each carrying four tons, plus brake van; in other words, a payload of 28 tons, or hardly more than one decent-sized lorry. It had some elegant if flimsy bogie coaches, quite the most handsome to run on any Welsh narrow gauge.

The Cambrian had taken over the railway even before it was opened, so it never had any real independence. It ran quietly and unremarkably as a rural branch line for 28 years, until in 1931 the passenger service succumbed to buses. The astonishing thing was that freight on the W&L kept going for so much longer, until 1956.

# NORTH WALES
# NARROW GAUGE RAILWAYS.

## SNOWDON AND BEDDGELERT DISTRICT.

THIS Railway (the gauge of which is only 2 feet) passes through some of the most picturesque scenery in Wales.

Starting from DINAS Station, 3 miles from Carnarvon, on the London and North Western Railway, the line ascends for 2 miles, at a gradient of 1 in 48, to TRYFAN JUNCTION, whence a Branch goes up to BRYNGWYN, rising for 2¼ miles at an average gradient of 1 in 40.

From BRYNGWYN a magnificent view is obtained, extending over Carnarvon, the Menai Straits, and Anglesey on the one hand, and to the fine mountains known as the Rivals (Yr Eifl) on the other; and the access to the top of Moel Tryfan is easy. This mountain is of great interest from the pre-historic sea-beach deposited on its summit, now 1400 feet above the sea level.

From TRYFAN JUNCTION the main Line runs through the Valley of BETTWS GARMON, following from WAENFAWR to RHYD-DDU, the same route as that taken by the coaches from Carnarvon to Beddgelert. In this valley there is a good stream for angling. Towards the head of the valley the mountains close in on either side. The scenery at this point becomes most picturesque; the Line winds in successive curves between the river on the left and the mountains on the right. Soon the waterfall and the old bridge of NANT MILL, well-known to artists, come into view on the left; and running close to the foot of the Great Mountain (MYNYDD MAWR) the Line shortly after emerges into the open space in which lies Lake Quellyn. Close to the lake on the right hand is the site of Wolf's Castle (CASTELL CIDWM). Here the Peak of Snowdon comes into sight.

Lake Quellyn is a beautiful expanse of water upwards of a mile in length and a quarter of a mile in width. It abounds with fish of all kinds; the fishing is free, and boats can be hired for fishing or excursions on the lake at the SNOWDON RANGER HOTEL, which is close to Snowdon Station.

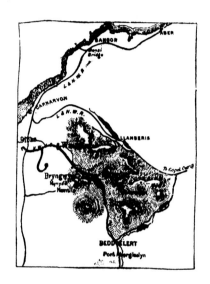

On reaching the lake the Line runs along the side of the sloping ground at the foot of the mountains, rising gradually to SNOWDON RANGER Station. There a fine view of Snowdon and its rugged precipices is obtained. The ascent can be made from this place, the distance being about 3 miles to the summit.

From SNOWDON RANGER Station to RHYD-DDU, the terminus, the Line ascends continuously. About a mile from Snowdon Ranger Station it crosses, by means of an iron bridge with a single span of 100 feet, a deep ravine, at the bottom of which flows a mountain stream, which descends in a cascade down the mountain side at the head of the gorge.

From this point the Line winds along the mountain side by rugged rocks and through wild scenery, not to be surpassed for its grandeur in Wales, until it reaches RHYD-DDU. The view of the lake in the distance from this portion of the Line, is very fine, and *can only be obtained from the Railway.*

The line is far above the level of the Lake and of the Coach Road; and the scene before the traveller by the Railway is grand and picturesque. Below lie the waters of Lake Quellyn; at its further end Mynydd Mawr stands boldly up; and across, on the opposite side, are seen the sharp peaks of the mountains which rise above and behind the lower range of hills which fringe the further edge of the lake.

**From RHYD-DDU the shortest ascent of Snowdon can be made, the distance to the summit being only 2¼ miles.**

RHYD-DDU is about three miles distance from Beddgelert, the road passes by the curious rock known as PITT'S HEAD; from its likeness to the profile of that eminent statesman.

Tourists by this Railway will have ample time to visit Beddgelert, the Grave of Gelert, and Pont Aberglaslyn, and returning the same route, or they can proceed by Coach to Llanberis, and thence to Carnarvon by London and North Western Railway, or proceed on to Portmadoc.

**Conveyances for Beddgelert meet the Trains on arrival at Rhyd-ddu,** as shown in time table below.

## TIME TABLE FOR JULY, AUGUST, SEPTEMBER, 1892.
### ALL TRAINS FIRST, SECOND AND THIRD CLASS.

Tourists should make sure of Cheap Coach Tickets for Beddgelert, by purchasing them before leaving Dinas.

| DOWN. | | 1,2,P. | Saturdays only. | | | | | Saturdays only. | Saturdays only. | |
|---|---|---|---|---|---|---|---|---|---|---|
| | | A.M. | A.M. | A.M. | A.M. | P.M. | P.M. | P.M. | P.M. | |
| CHESTER .... depart | | | | 6 0 | 10 0 | | 2 20 | | | |
| RHYL " | | | | 7 13 | 10 43 | | | | | |
| ABERGELE " | | | | 7 23 | 10 51 | | | | | |
| COLWYN BAY " | | | | 7 43 | 11 4 | | | | | |
| LLANDUDNO " | | | | 7 49 | 11 0 | | | | | |
| P'MAENMAWR " | | | | 8 12 | 11 31 | | | | | |
| L'FAIRFECHAN " | | | | 8 18 | 11 38 | | | | | |
| BANGOR " | | | | 8 54 | 12 5 | | 4 10 | 5 15 | 7 25 | |
| CARNARVON " | | | | 9 25 | 12 35 | 3 0 | 4 45 | 6 45 | 8 21 | |
| DINAS arrive | | | | 9 35 | 12 45 | 3 10 | 4 55 | 6 55 | 8 21 | |
| DINAS depart | 6 0 | 7 45 | 9 40 | 12 47 | 3 12 | 5 0 | 7 0 | 8 25 | | |
| TRYFAN JUNCT. arrive | 6 9 | 7 55 | 9 50 | 12 56 | 3 21 | 5 10 | 7 9 | 8 35 | | |
| TRYFAN JUN. depart | | | 7 0 | 9 52 | 1259 | 3 24 | 5 12 | 7 10 | 8 37 | |
| RHOSTRYFAN " | | | 8 4 | 9 58 | 1 0 | 5 30 | 5 18 | 7 15 | 8 43 | |
| BRYNGWYN arrive | | | 8 15 | 10 6 | 1 15 | 3 40 | 5 28 | 7 24 | 8 53 | |
| WAENFAWR depart | 6 18 | | 10 0 | 1 5 | 3 30 | 5 20 | | 8 45 | | |
| BETTWS GARMON " | 6 23 | | 10 5 | 1 10 | 3 35 | 5 25 | | 8 50 | | |
| SNOWDON RANGER " | 6 36 | | 10 18 | 1 23 | 3 47 | 5 38 | | | | |
| RHYD-DDU arrive | 6 50 | | 10 31 | 1 36 | 4 0 | 5 51 | | | | |
| BEDDGELERT (BY COACH) Arrive about | | | 11 15 | 2 15 | 4 30 | 6 30 | | | | |

| UP. | Saturdays excepted. | Saturdays only. | 1,2,P. | | | | | Saturdays only. |
|---|---|---|---|---|---|---|---|---|
| | A.M. | A.M. | A.M. | P.M. | P.M. | P.M. | P.M. | P.M. |
| BEDDGELERT (Depart by Coach) | | | 9 40 | 12 50 | 3 10 | | 6 10 | |
| RHYD-DDU .... depart | 7 20 | 8 20 | 10 35 | 1 45 | 4 5 | | 7 5 | |
| SNOWD'N RANGER " | 7 34 | 8 33 | 10 48 | 1 59 | 4 17 | | 7 18 | |
| BETTWS GARMON " | 7 47 | 8 46 | 11 1 | 2 12 | 4 29 | | 7 31 | 8 55 |
| WAENFAWR " | 7 53 | 8 51 | 11 5 | 2 17 | 4 34 | | 7 36 | 9 0 |
| BRYNGWYN depart | | 8 35 | 10 50 | 2 0 | 4 17 | 5 35 | | 8 55 |
| RHOSTRYFAN " | | 8 43 | 11 0 | 2 10 | 4 27 | 5 45 | | 9 4 |
| TRYFAN JUNCT'N arr. | | 8 49 | 11 5 | 2 15 | 4 32 | 5 50 | | 9 10 |
| TRYFAN JUNCT'N dep. | 8 3 | 9 0 | 11 15 | 2 27 | 4 42 | 5 52 | 7 45 | 9 10 |
| DINAS arrive | 8 13 | 9 10 | 11 24 | 2 37 | 4 51 | 6 0 | 7 55 | 9 20 |
| DINAS depart | 8 14 | 9 13 | 11 25 | 2 42 | 5 20 | | 7 59 | 7 59 |
| CARNARVON arrive | 8 26 | 9 24 | 11 38 | 2 55 | 5 32 | | 8 10 | 8 10 |
| BANGOR " | 8 59 | 10 15 | 12 4 | 3 22 | 5 57 | | 8 44 | 8 44 |
| L'FAIRFECHAN " | 9 25 | 10 51 | 12 51 | | 6 22 | | | 9 45 |
| P'MAENMAWR " | 9 33 | 10 59 | 12 59 | | 6 29 | | | 9 52 |
| LLANDUDNO " | 10 24 | 11 35 | 1 25 | | 7 0 | | 9 47 | 10 25 |
| COLWYN BAY " | 10 7 | 11 35 | 1 30 | | 7 8 | | | 10 40 |
| ABERGELE " | 10 20 | 11 58 | 1 42 | | 7 24 | | | 10 59 |
| RHYL " | 10 30 | 12 9 | 1 51 | | 7 34 | | 10 0 | 11 10 |
| CHESTER " | 11 24 | 1 5 | 2 35 | | 8 19 | | 10 50 | |

### FARES FROM CARNARVON.

| | SINGLE. | | | RETURN. | | |
|---|---|---|---|---|---|---|
| | 1st. | 2nd. | P'rly | 1st. | 2nd. | P'rly |
| | s. d. | s. d. | s. d. | s. d. | s. d. | s. d. |
| TRYFAN JUNCT. | 0 7 | 0 5 | | 1 0 | 0 10 | 0 10 |
| RHOSTRYFAN | 0 9 | 0 5½ | | 1 8 | 1 3 | 0 11 |
| BRYNGWYN | 1 0 | 0 7 | | 2 0 | 1 5 | 1 2 |
| WAENFAWR | 0 9 | 0 5½ | | 1 0 | 1 3 | 0 11 |
| BETTWS GARMON | 1 0 | 0 7 | | 2 2 | 1 6 | 1 2 |
| SNOWDON RANGER | 1 4 | 0 10 | | 3 0 | 2 3 | 1 8 |
| RHYD-DDU | 1 8 | 1 0½ | | 3 6 | 2 9 | 2 1 |
| BEDDGELERT | | | | | | |

### FARES FROM DINAS.

| To | SINGLE. | | | RETURN. | | |
|---|---|---|---|---|---|---|
| | 1st. | 2nd. | 3rd. | 1st. | 2nd. | 3rd. |
| | s. d. | s. d. | s. d. | s. d. | s. d. | s. d. |
| TRYFAN JUNCT. | 0 5 | 0 4 | 0 3 | 0 10 | 0 6 | 0 5 |
| RHOSTRYFAN | 0 6 | 0 5 | 0 3 | 0 10 | 0 7 | 0 6 |
| BRYNGWYN | 0 10 | 0 8 | 0 6 | 1 4 | 1 0 | 0 10 |
| WAENFAWR | 0 5 | 0 4 | 0 3 | 0 10 | 0 7 | 0 6 |
| BETTWS GARMON | 0 6 | 0 5 | 0 4 | 1 0 | 0 10 | 0 8 |
| SNOWDON RANGER | 1 3 | 1 0 | 0 7½ | 2 3 | 1 9 | 1 0 |
| RHYD-DDU | 1 7 | 1 3 | 0 9½ | 2 9 | 2 2 | 1 0 |
| BEDDGELERT | 2 4 | 2 0 | 1 6½ | 4 0 | 3 5 | 3 0 |

CONDITIONS—The arrival time denotes when trains may be expected. The Directors give notice that the Company do not undertake that the trains shall start or arrive at the time specified in the Time Bills, nor will they be answerable for any loss, inconvenience, or injury, which may arise from delays or detention; but attention will be paid to ensure punctuality, as far as practicable. The Published Time Bills of the Company are only intended to fix the time at which Passengers may be certain to obtain their Tickets for any journey from the various Stations.

The granting Tickets to Passengers to places off the Company's Lines is an arrangement made for the greater convenience of the public; but the Company do not hold themselves responsible for any delay, detention, or other loss, or injury whatsoever arising off their Lines, or from the acts or defaults of other parties, nor for the correctness of the times on other Lines or Companies, nor for the arrival of this Company's own Trains in time for the nominally corresponding Train of any other Company or party.

Passengers can book from Dinas through to Beddgelert. Tickets, which include the Rail, and Coach Fares can only be purchased at Dinas Station. **Rail and Coach Fares, Dinas to Beddgelert and back,**
**1st Class 4s., 2nd Class 3s. 6d., and 3rd Class 3s.**

The shortest and best ascent of Snowdon is made from Rhyd-ddu, the distance to the summit being only 2¼ miles, against 5 miles, from Llanberis. **Rhyd-ddu Station is situated on the** side of Snowdon itself, and the path leads directly from it. Guides meet all Trains.

Passengers change carriages at Dinas to and from Carnarvon by London and North Western Railway.

## TRAINS DO NOT RUN ON SUNDAYS.

**S. TANNER,**
SECRETARY & MANAGER.

Station, near Carnarvon, June 25, 1892.
smith, Printer, Llandudno.

Daily except Sundays one train ran each way, usually with the statutory seven truckloads of coal and little else but a few parcels in the van. On Mondays there was often a second run, taking sheep or cattle to Welshpool market; sometimes there was enough coal or other traffic to warrant a second trip on other days as well, but not very often. Finally BR gave a twitch and realised it was all a nonsense, and closed it. But except for the first mile through Welshpool, where the track threaded its way between the houses and over the roads at odd blind angles, it is all still there; in 1963 the line was taken over by preservationists and now runs passenger trains once more, hauled by a remarkable assortment of engines and rolling stock imported from Europe, Africa and the West Indies.

Wales had a greater number and variety of narrow-gauge railways than any other part of Britain, and it is extraordinary how many of them survive. Indeed there are now several new ones, opened during the 1980s on derelict ex-BR formations; at Bala on part of the Ruabon–Barmouth line, on part of the Newcastle Emlyn branch, and at Pontsticill Junction on the old Brecon & Merthyr. In addition, the Llanberis Lake Railway runs on part of the old four-foot gauge Padarn line. But most Welsh lines always have been rather small-scale affairs, carrying tiny flows of traffic with equipment that was not very impressive or interesting. The Festiniog certainly played a part in a world context a century ago, when it

*Great Western Railway (Welshpool & Llanfair section). Beyer Peacock 0–6–0 tank No 822 (ex W&LR No 1)* The Earl *(BP 3496/03) at Llanfair Caereinion station with a train for Welshpool on 9 June 1925.* A.W. Croughton

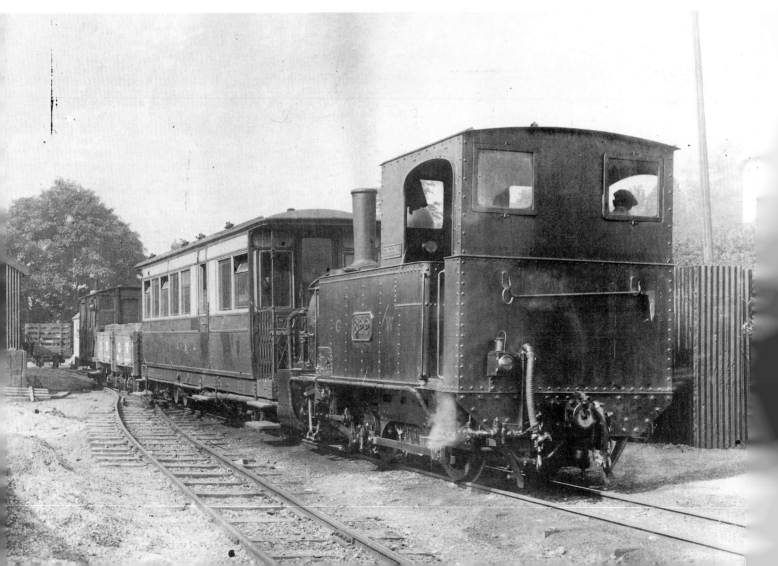

demonstrated how with boldness and ingenuity a 2ft gauge line could perform a useful function, economically and profitably, in the world as it was then; and if a two-footer, then how much more so a line of 2ft 6in, 3ft, or 3ft 6in gauge. The FR had a part in the origins of that very large proportion of the world's railways built to a gauge narrower than standard.

But for the rest, why the fuss? Perhaps there are two things worth thinking of. There is of course always the charm of the small, the odd, the self-contained and complete, particularly when it is sited in a beautiful place, as most of these lines were. But there is also the point that the surviving lines, or most of them, have found a new and equally genuine purpose. In a state where the main-line railway network has been modernised, computerised, dehumanised and in the name of some kind of accountant's dream of efficiency made so remote and perfect and costly and useless a thing that there is some doubt as to the point of allowing it to continue to exist and, where in the name of tidiness and concentration all the small stations and sidings have been done away with, so that customers seeking rail transport are directed to efficient road-rail transfer points so distant that they might just as well remain with their cars and lorries until, in an island the size of Britain, they get to where they were intending to go in the first place, it is good to be reminded that there was a time when industry and machines all had a local relevance and operated on a scale where a person could understand, participate, and make some individual contribution. More employment offered is in central offices or works or costly miracles of remote control, so that the unavoidable intrusion of tracks and trains in the green country is coming to be seen as a minor nuisance contributing nothing to the locality where similarly more of industry is going the same sort of way. One sort of activity is for men, the other is for robots.

*A goods train from Llanfair Caereinion is halted at Seven Stars, Welshpool on 4 June 1953. Parked vehicles were always a problem in these congested places and the crew have left 0–6–0 tank No 822 to remove a car from their right of way. This section through the town from Welshpool Station to Raven Square remained after closure in 1956 but was excluded from the lease to the preservation company and was abandoned some five years later.*
J.C. Flemons

*Running a narrow-gauge tourist railway is far from a matter of 'old men playing trains', as was once claimed in the High Court. It also involves hard construction work. Here repairs are being carried out to the Dolgoch Viaduct on the Talyllyn Railway, during the winter period when no public trains were running.* Talyllyn Railway Company

*Very much a picture of today's modern tourist railway. A Festiniog Railway Father Christmas special making its wintry way towards Blaenau Festiniog behind two one time Penrhyn Railway 0–4–0s,* Blanche *and* Linda. *There is virtually nothing of the old FR in this train – locomotives acquired to bolster up an overworked and inadequate (by numbers) fleet of local residents and rebuilt to serve the railway's requirements, plus totally new and rebuilt coaching stock. The Festiniog regards itself, quite properly, not only as a railway rescued from the dead but also one reconstituted to meet modern needs. It is one of Wales' premier tourist attractions.* N.F. Gurley

Of course, the main point of keeping the remaining Welsh narrow-gauge lines is not to give pleasure and fulfilment to the people who work on them; it has primarily to be to provide an enjoyable experience for their riders and patrons. Fortunately this seems to be being achieved. Railways used to be enjoyable to ride on; these still are.

# CHAPTER FOUR
# IRELAND

The situation of narrow-gauge railways in Ireland was radically different from those in England, Scotland and Wales. There were many more of them, in the first place, eventually a total of 14 public passenger-carrying lines, with a total of 530 route-miles between them. All were of 3ft gauge, and were generally much more substantially built. on the other hand, they came late; the first was not opened until 1875. Most were built within a fairly short period, as the result of government policy which applied during that time only; all are now closed. Not a single yard remains of any of them.

*Londonderry & Lough Swilly Railway 4–6–0 tank No 3 waits to leave Newtowncunningham with a goods train for Londonderry in 1952. The railway closed completely the following year when the remaining traffic was transferred to the road transport fleet operated by the railway.* P.B. Whitehouse

Quite apart from the question of narrow-gauge lines; the whole policy of government in Ireland in relation to railways was radically different compared with Britain, even though Britain and Ireland were united under one Parliament for the whole period of railway construction. Ireland was poor and thinly inhabited, and had very little industry and almost no mining. Matters were steadily getting worse, as the level of population declined for the whole of the 19th century, largely because of emigration to the English cities of people for whom there was no work and sometimes little food in Ireland. In Britain the whole railway network was built, operated, and maintained by private capital without any significant assistance from the State or even local government. There was provision for some state money to be put towards the construction of light railways later, particularly under the 1896 Light Railway Act, but this was very little applied and the only narrow-gauge line in Britain which received this kind of help was the Welsh Highland. In Ireland, however, matters were quite different, since at the start government despaired of getting railways built unless it found some of the money itself; indeed it was even prepared to assist with the construction of the Dublin-Cork trunk line in the 1840s. Policy varied somewhat depending on what government was in power in London, some of them taking a robust and unsympathetic view. Under a statute of 1835 the Irish Board of Works had power to lend government money to assist railway building (and other works of improvement) where other finance could not be found, and this power was very widely used. By 1880 therefore the Irish railway network was tolerably complete and many lines had been built which never would have found birth unaided. But some areas still lacked railways and arguably needed them, and the Tramways Act of 1883 was intended to get them built.

Before 1883 only three narrow-gauge lines had been built in Ireland, all close together in the extreme north-eastern corner. First was the Ballymena, Cushendall and Red Bay (which never actually reached either Cushendall or Red Bay), a 16½ mile line from Ballymena on the Belfast–Coleraine–Londonderry main line of the Belfast & Northern Counties Railway, to Parkmore and Retreat, opened in 1875–6. It climbed into a remote part of the Antrim Mountains – it was in fact the highest railway in all Ireland – and its objective was some iron ore workings. Passenger business was quite secondary, and indeed not catered for at all until 1886, after the B&NC had taken over. By that time Ballymena had been reached by another narrow-gauge line, the Ballymena & Larne, opened in 1877–9. This company, which operated over 31 miles of route, including a six-mile branch, served a more prosperous area and indeed formed part of a useful through route to Londonderry from the ferry port of Larne, considerably shorter than the main line via Greenisland and Belfast, so much so in fact, that after the B&NC took over the B&L, in turn in 1899, a through connection was provided by one of the very rare examples of an express train to run on any narrow-gauge line in the British Isles. The third early Irish

narrow gauge was the Ballycastle, from Ballymoney (a few miles north of Ballymena) to the town of its name, 16 miles long and opened in 1880.

All these railways had been built very largely with the aid of cheap loans from the Board of Works. The 1883 Act left the authority to make these loans intact, but brought in a new financial system and a new philosophy. The new system was to give railway promoters, once their schemes had been approved, authority to issue shares on which dividends would be guaranteed, partly by the central government and partly by the local authorities, and therefore the ratepayers, of the districts served. They could also raise loans on which interest and repayment were both guaranteed in the same way; finally, the local authorities (with some central government help) were held bound to make good any deficit in working that the railway companies concerned might suffer. The new philosophy was that there should be a presumption, on the grounds that government had been persuaded that it would save money, that any new railways to be built with this financial assistance should generally be of 3ft gauge. Of the 433 miles of railway built under this Act, all but 170 were therefore narrow; there is no real evidence of any careful criterion being applied to decide the gauge in any case, and one is left with the impression that the promoters could have broad gauge if they argued for it, and that the better-advised ones did so.

Central government had certainly intended to be generous in the 1883 Act, and to see a lot of new railways built. In both these objects they succeeded, but all the same the legislation was ill-considered and had several unfortunate consequences. On the technical side, for instance, the economy which had been hoped for by favouring the narrow gauge was not achieved. In hilly and difficult terrain the use of narrow gauge would achieve maximum savings in construction, but many of the new lines were in much easier country where these savings were insignificant, particularly as very often the narrow-gauge locomotives had to be very nearly as large as many broad-gauge ones. The expense and inconvenience of transhipment of freight at the break-of-gauge points was also overlooked.

More serious were the financial and political drawbacks. The total amount of guaranteed share capital was fixed at the outset. Where the promoters had accurately judged the cost of the railway and nothing went wrong, all was well and good; the line got built and properly equipped, had a fair start in life, and the intentions of the Act could be fulfilled. But sometimes the promoters of the railway underestimated the money they would need, and sometimes the promoters got it right, but the government and local authorities got it wrong and reduced the guaranteed capital below what was needed to do a proper job. Either way, the railway then had to be skimped, in grades, curves, stations and signalling, size and power of locomotives, quantity of rolling stock, weight of rail and quantity of ballast, or sometimes all of these things, which meant a pretty disastrous start. Another thing that sometimes went wrong was that even with a guaranteed 5 per cent dividend, in some cases the shares could only be sold at a discount, so the budgeted cash was never raised.

Once the line had been built, the shareholders appointed a majority of the directors and could then lie back and enjoy their guaranteed dividends come what may, and even if the railway went to rack and ruin. The shareholders' directors could always outvote the representatives of the local authorities on the company boards. The only remedy the latter had was that if they were called to make good operating losses in more than two successive years, they could dismiss the board and appoint a Committee of Management to run the railway (but the shareholders still got their dividends). There was not much likelihood that the local authorities would make a better fist of the job than the original directors had, and they still had to pay up, so this was not much of a remedy. In short, the whole situation was a potential minefield.

A number of new railways were already in the promotion or construction stage while Parliament was considering the 1883 Act, and thus it did not apply to them fully. One was the Castlederg & Victoria Bridge, a seven-mile line opened in 1884 in County Omagh, a roadside tramway which had a barely profitable operating record but which was hamstrung throughout its life because it was never able to obtain the adequate financing the Act would have made possible. Two more were largely or wholly financed without government help, but deserve special mention because they were both very early electric railways.

The three-mile Bessbrook & Newry, opened in 1885, picked up its current, at 245 volts, from a centre third rail, but had short lengths of overhead wire at level crossings, with bow collectors on the motor coaches, to prevent trains from becoming gapped. It ran quite uneventfully until it closed in 1948, but had one unique feature; its track was laid throughout with double rails, so that although its passenger stock had ordinary railway wheels its freight wagons had plain unflanged ones, like those on early plateways, and could be hauled by horses along the ordinary roads at each end of the line. It also had its own hydro-electric generating station, as did the other line, the Giant's Causeway Portrush & Bush Valley, an eight-mile line opened between 1883 and 1887. This also used 245 volts, but at the start and until 1899 the current was collected from a side third rail. Public outcry and the general fear of widespread electrocution, to the company's dismay, caused this third rail to be prohibited on the mile or so of street running through Portrush, and so steam tram locomotives had to he used on this length until the overhead wires went up (and in fact they remained in service to assist on peak days until 1915). Public alarm remained very vocal, even so, when the time came for electric traction to be inaugurated – bear in mind that this was one of the very first electric railways in the world – so that on opening day the chairman of the company, determined to stop any further trouble, ceremonially sat down on the live rail before the assembled crowd and made a lengthy speech while in that position. Entirely reassured, the throng then climbed aboard the trains and sped off smokelessly to Bushmills, while the chairman, having waved them off, limped home to have some nasty burns seen to. A rare and noble example of devotion beyond the call of corporate duty. It was sad that, having survived so long and become a really amazing museum piece, complete with its original power station, the Giant's Causeway line was closed and scrapped in 1949.

The other two 3ft gauge railways in the pipeline around 1882 each formed part of the two neighbouring systems in County Donegal, in the north-west corner of Ireland, that became far and away the two largest and most important narrow-gauge railway

*Coat of Arms Castlederg & Victoria Bridge Tramway Company.*
A.W. Croughton

*Castlederg & Victoria Bridge Tramway. Cattle train behind 2–6–0 tank No 4 with skirts partly removed, date not known but probably around 1924. No 4 was fitted with skirts on one side (left) of the locomotive only; it worked chimney first towards Castlederg and the line ran only on the northern side of the roadway.*
Millbrook House collection

*Giant's Causeway, Portrush & Bush Valley Railway and Tramway. Steam tram engine and train in the days before electric traction. Note the two classes of four-wheeled coaches.* L&GRP

undertakings in the British Isles. As well as being close together (and connected), they had a rather similar history.

The Finn Valley Railway, opened in 1863, was a 13-mile 5ft 3in gauge branch which connected with the Great Northern of Ireland's main Portadown to Londonderry line at Strabane and headed off in the direction of the hills of Donegal, but through easy country, to the town of Stranorlar. It had a placid but not very rewarding existence in this not very busy area, and it was felt that things would be better if the line extended westwards. But the idea of saving construction cost by adopting the narrow gauge for this extension was seductive and ultimately the company was seduced; so it was as a 3ft gauge line that the associated Donegal Railway pushed westwards over the Barnesmore Gap, for 14 miles, to a dot on the map called Lough Eske. There in 1882 the railway halted because the money had run out, and it was not for some years, in fact until 1889, that it reached its first objective, the town of Donegal, four miles further on, with the aid of guaranteed share and loan capital raised under the provisions of the 1883 Act. Meanwhile further plans for extension hung fire; indeed the delays caused by the confused situation at Lough Eske meant that with this one small exception the Donegal system was not developed under the 1883 Act, but the rather more generous 1889 legislation. For some years the break of gauge remained at Stranorlar, but following the amalgamation of the Finn Valley and Donegal companies in 1892 the older line was narrowed and the transhipment point moved to Strabane.

The situation of the Londonderry & Lough Swilly Railway was almost identical. This was a 14-mile 5ft 3in gauge line also opened in 1863, from its own station at Londonderry (Graving Dock) to Buncrana. Soon after, another company was formed to build a 5ft 3in gauge branch from Tooban Junction on the L&LS over the 19 miles to Letterkenny, but the contractor made away with the money and for nearly 20 years the Letterkenny Railway had the embarrassment of owning a nearly complete line of cuttings and embankments, but no track. Ultimately the Board of Works came to the rescue with a loan (which was never repaid), but insisted that the line should be built to the narrow gauge. This fateful step taken, the Letterkenny Railway was at last opened in 1883; the Lough Swilly put up with the transhipment at Tooban Junction for a couple of years, and then seeing the greater nonsense of a break of gauge just six miles outside Londonderry, converted its own railway to a 3ft gauge in 1885. One feels they did so against their better judgement; certainly although the L&LS took over the operation of the Letterkenny line from the start, it never absorbed the Letterkenny company, which remained independent (and indebted) to the end. The Lough Swilly was also mistrustful of all government bodies, Railway Commissioners, Boards of Works, and in the years to come proved to be a great thorn in the flesh of all civil servants. This, as we shall see, did it no harm at all; indeed the Lough Swilly story is the only one in Irish narrow-gauge railway history to have any kind of happy ending. But during the 1880s both the Swilly and the Donegal were short narrow-gauge lines, originally broad, with considerable extensions proposed to serve the whole beautiful but poverty-stricken County of Donegal, until then largely rail-less.

In the rest of Ireland the 1883 Act produced an absolute banquet of railway projects. It seemed as if nothing could go wrong; a lot of useful and necessary lines would be built, and the people who put up the money were sure of getting a good return on it because of the government guarantee. As we have already noticed, there were some potential flaws, and worse followed, but none of this was evident at the start. No fewer than six separate narrow-gauge railway companies were promoted under the Act, and opened their lines during the next few years, as well as nine broad-gauge projects.

The first was the Schull & Skibbereen, a 15-mile concern in the remoter regions of West Cork, opened in 1886. It rapidly demonstrated most of the things that could go wrong. The original estimate of the cost of building the line had been reduced at the behest of government, and then a lot of capital never came in because the shares had to be sold at a discount. The railway as built was therefore skimped, with light rail and excessive curves and gradients (as steep as 1 in 22); to make matters worse small and underpowered but cheap locomotives were provided, which constantly broke down. Disastrous losses resulted, and the ratepayers were left to support the burden of a railway which was almost useless. After two years of this, the original directors were removed under the Act, a Committee of Management appointed by the local authorities, and things slowly were pulled round, but only with the investment of much more money and purchase of a new stock of locomotives. The

*Schull & Skibbereen Light Railway. A mixed train poses on the viaduct at Ballydehob, Co Cork around the turn of the century, possibly in 1906.*
National Library, Dublin

line always ran at a loss, and around 1910 had settled down to costing the local ratepayers up to 1s 2½d (6p) in the pound in subsidies, a fairly heavy sum and in fact the third heaviest in Ireland. But at least they had quite a useful train service.

Next came the Cavan & Leitrim, a much more respectable concern. This had a main line of 33 miles from Dromod, on the Mullingar-Sligo main line, to Belturbet, terminus of a branch of the Great Northern, together with a 15-mile branch from Ballinamore to Arigna. It raised enough money, and opened uneventfully in 1887–8 with a reasonably well-built and well-equipped railway

which soon settled down and generally earned enough to meet its operating expenses. However profits were not large enough to pay dividends, so the ratepayers had to pay up under the guarantee, if not very much. This did not avert evil. Because the railway met its operating costs, the directors were impregnable and unsackable under the Act; but because the local authorities believed, or said they believed, that they had originally agreed to underwrite the railway because the directors had told them it was going to be a gold mine, they wailed very long and loud about it. There was a further cause of aggravation in the fact that one of Ireland's few coal mines came to be established in the hills some four miles from Arigna station, and the directors of the C&L, very public-spiritedly put up their own personal money to get this colliery going. Clearly it would do much better if the railway were extended to the pithead, but the local authorities were not having any of that. Once bitten twice shy; either the villainous capitalists found their own money again, or they could put up with packhorses to get the coal to the station. The price of coal thus remained high and uncompetitive with imported Welsh coal, but a most satisfying and enjoyable quarrel was thereby kept going. In fact the Arigna Mines extension was not built until wartime pressures forced the issue, and it opened in 1920. One thing may however be said in the local authorities' favour; even though their guarantee was only called on to cover dividends and not losses, the cost of the C&L, in relation to the wealth of the area was so considerable that supporting it added about 1s 6d (7½p) in the pound to the rates, more even than the Schull & Skibbereen. Thus a better-built and more profitable railway was actually more of a burden than a skimped and loss-making one – not a consequence foreseen at Westminster.

The next line to be opened was the Clogher Valley, a rather less ambitious and for the most part roadside affair. This ran for 37 miles from Tynan to Maguiresbridge, both stations on the Great Northern, via the market towns of Aughnacloy and Fivemiletown. It had a placid history by Irish narrow-gauge standards; in fact its promoters seemed to have got it about right. It was built soundly but not extravagantly; its locomotives were small and simple but adequate for their task. Its traffic was pretty light, since it met the broad gauge at both ends and served nothing very important between, and it generally lost a modest amount each year, but it ran smoothly and the total load on the rates was quite small, particularly as it ran through a rather richer area.

For a long time the Cork & Muskerry Light Railway was the most successful result of the 1883 Act. This was a much smaller concern, starting from its own terminus in Cork (Western Road) and running, partly on the roadside and in Cork itself in the middle of the road, 15½ miles to Coachford, with a three-mile branch to Blarney, all opened once again in 1887–8. In 1893 an eight-mile extension was opened from St Anne's on the Blarney branch to Donoughmore. Partly because its traffic was semi-suburban, and swollen by the masses of tourists and orators going to kiss the

Opposite:
*The hub of the Cavan & Leitrim was at Ballinamore. Standing in the shed yard on 24 June 1955 were left to right:- Ex Tralee & Dingle 2–6–2 tank No 5T with 2–6–0 tank No 3T alongside but behind Cavan & Leitrim 4–4–0 tank No 4L. C&L 4–4–0 tanks 8L and 2L complete the picture. Tralee & Dingle 5L was fortunately purchased for preservation in the USA when the line closed in 1959. It has since returned to Tralee where it is the centre of attraction on a short rebuilt section of the original line. P.W. Gray.*

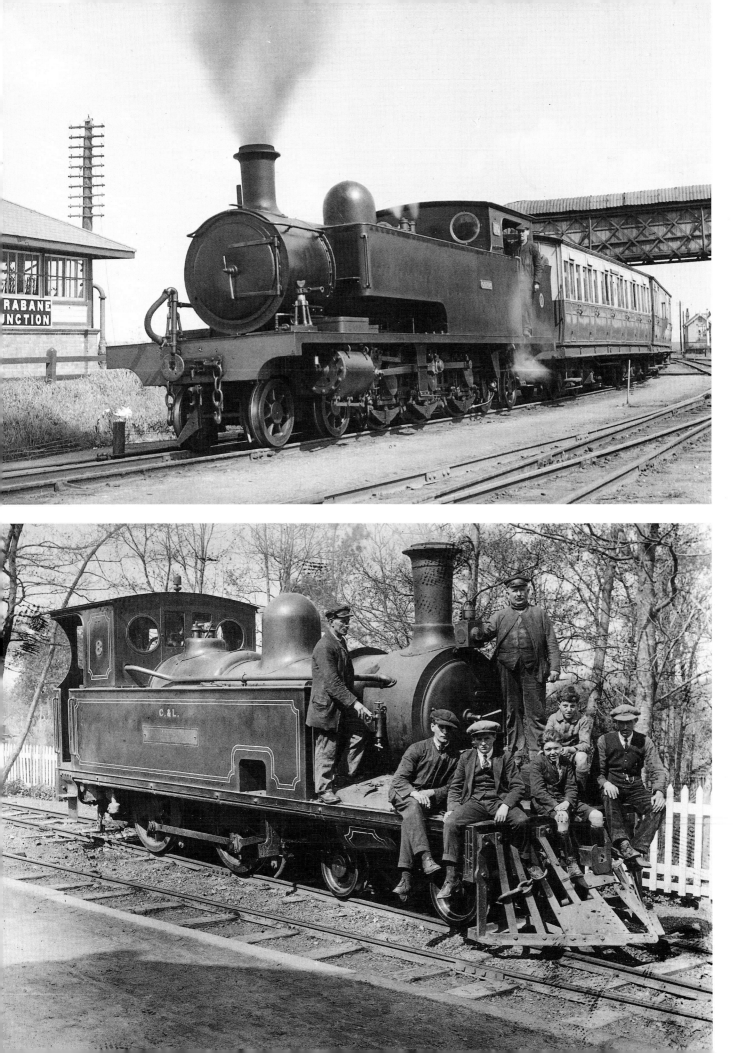

*A real 'Irish' train. Clougher Valley Railway Tractor No 2 waits with a train at Fivemiletown on 12 May 1937. R.G. Jarvis*

Blarney Stone, the C&M in the years up to 1914 ran at a fair profit and indeed was generally able to contribute something towards payment of its own dividends, so its burden on the rates was only small. It was certainly unique among Irish narrow-gauge railways in another way, because Blarney trains actually shared tracks with the Cork electric trams for some distance. But when motor buses came into the picture later, things of course changed.

The most important 3ft gauge railway produced by the 1883 Act, was the West Clare. It ran for 27 miles from the junction with the broad gauge at Ennis to Miltown Malbay, a pleasant town on the coast with some pretensions as a holiday resort. It puffed through pleasantly hilly but not unduly difficult country, and was substantially built and equipped, as can be judged from the fact that its 27 miles required a total guaranteed capital of £217,000 compared with the £176,000 spent on the 37-mile Clogher Valley. The South Clare Railway, an extension of 21 miles from Miltown Malbay to Kilkee, with a four-mile branch from Moyasta Junction to Kilrush, also served some seaside towns with pretensions to gentility; but while the WCR usually managed to make a small profit in those years, the SCR generally ran at a modest loss. This was hardly surprising since the WC's traffic was increased by the SC's contribution to it; since the latter was an extension, this did not operate in reverse. The two lines were always worked as one. The complete 'West Clare' was thus in fact not a bad little railway, offering quite a good service with few real problems. Its misfortune was to have to carry the kind of clientele it had, travelling to prosperous middle-class holiday villas on the coast and not disposed to put up with mixed trains which paused at various stations along the way to

*Opposite:*
*County Donegal Railways Joint Committee 4-6-4 tank No 10 Owena leaves Strabane for Stranorlar on 14 April 1937. The locomotives were a very plain shade of red whilst the coaching stock was resplendent in a red and cream livery – not unlike that used by BR shortly after nationalisation! R.G. Jarvis*

*Cavan and Leitrim 4-4-0 tank No 8 Queen Victoria at Dromod on 17 May 1924. Dromod was the interchange point with the 5ft 3in Dublin–Sligo main line of the Midland Great Western Railway. A.W. Croughton*

101

*A misty day at Blarney, Great Southern Railways (Cork & Muskerry Light Railway section). 4–4–0 tank No 7K (formerly Peaks) on the 12.05pm Cork (Western Road) to Donoughamore (via Blarney) on 7 October 1933. A.W. Croughton*

shunt wagons off and on. Ultimately the West Clare made the mistake of selling a ticket to one Percy French (they should have poked him into a horse and cart), a music-hall star who wrote a rude song about it which across the ages echoes still. Peasants would have suffered in silence; alone among the Irish narrow gauges, the West Clare transported the bourgeoisie, who squealed like pigs at the very minor inconveniences it sometimes offered. They also faithfully recorded every Irishism perpetrated by its staff, of which one famous example was provided by the guard of a mixed train who put his name to the telegram in which he economically reported a minor shunting derailment to headquarters at Ennis – 'Off Again On Again Gone Again Finnigan'.

There was, though, a limit beyond which even the peasants would revolt; and this limit was gaily waltzed far beyond by the Tralee & Dingle, blackest sheep of all the motley flock to result from the 1883 Act. The main line of this disreputable concern joined the two towns of its name, 31 miles apart, and it had a six-mile branch from Castlegregory Junction to Castlegregory. It was all opened for business in 1891, and in spite of the fact that it crossed and followed a range of mountains for most of its length, its total capital, all guaranteed, was only £120,000. Compare this with the rather lightly-built Clogher Valley, the same length and in much easier country, which cost £176,000 to build and equip. The Tralee & Dingle was built on the cheap to a degree that was astounding, even allowing for the fact that most of the track was on the roadside (where it had a murderous habit of swerving from one side of the road to the other without cause or excuse and little warning). Almost the only thing that was not skimped was in fact the locomotives, which while insufficient in number were adequate in power. On the other hand, even the directors of the Tralee & Dingle could appreciate that on a line with the heaviest sustained gradients in Ireland, including four miles of 1 in 30 and worse from Castlegregory Junction to the summit at Glenagalt, power was essential. As a result, economies had to be made in other directions, notably staffing. The first couple of years of operation on the T&D was a black comedy rivalling anything that had happened on the Schull & Skibbereen, and including boilers ruined through ignorance and inattention of the half-trained footplate crews. Employees were so few that the Locomotive Engineer, as well as maintaining the fleet more or less single-handed, was expected to drive on busy days, and in 1893 this unfortunate and inexperienced officer was responsible for a disastrous runaway and pile-up. To save steam, he had not coupled up the brakes. Needless to say the company's insurance did not cover the damage and the unfortunate ratepayers had to shell out not only for the continuous heavy operating losses, not only for the guaranteed dividends, but also in compensation. Once the original board of directors had been sacked and a Committee of Management put in, things improved slowly, and by 1910 the Tralee & Dingle was only adding 2s 4d (11½p) in the pound to the local rates – still considerably the heaviest burden of any Irish railway. Things got worse again later, when the area was much affected by the 'troubles', and in 1922 it was costing the local ratepayers no less than 9s 2d (46p) in the pound.

Long before these goings-on, however, government had come to realise that all was not well and several further and better Acts were passed in 1889, 1893 and 1896 to remedy matters. One change was that the burden of the guarantees on the local authorities was reduced by the central government announcing its preparedness, for the first time, to make outright free grants of money with which to build approved railways, grants which could and did on occasion amount to 100 per cent, although usually they were somewhat less. The other reform was that the presumption in favour of the narrow gauge for all new railways was dropped; as a result, apart from cases of extensions of existing lines, and with one other exception, no more narrow-gauge lines were built.

The extensions, however, were fairly considerable, and all to the two Donegal systems we have already noticed. The Donegal Railway was extended for 19 miles from Donegal to Killybegs in 1893, with the aid of a 100 per cent capital grant, and on the same basis the 24-mile branch from Stranorlar to Glenties was opened in 1895. A further extension, 14½ miles from Strabane to Londonderry (Victoria Road) was opened in 1900, giving the Donegal access without break of gauge to the principal city of the north-west and its major traffic objective; for this reason it was supposed to be commercially self-sustaining and no state finance was given for that line, nor for the last extension to the Donegal system, the 15½ miles from Donegal to Ballyshannon, opened in 1905. The predictable result of this was that the Donegal company got into difficulties and had to be rescued by being taken over jointly by the Great Northern (of Ireland) and the Midland (of England). The Derby octopus had extended a tentacle into the north of Ireland with the acquisition of the Belfast & Northern Counties in 1906, and got a rude shock when that tentacle was grasped and hauled right across to the Atlantic coast. To make matters worse, the GNR(I) refused to have anything to do with the Strabane–Derry line, parallel to its own route, and the Midland's Northern Counties Committee had to take this on unaided. However, the newly-established County Donegal Railways Joint Committee settled down well enough and became responsible for the largest, and arguably best-run, 3ft gauge system in Ireland. When it took over the working of the newly-opened and legally independent 19-mile Strabane & Letterkenny Railway in 1909, and including the Londonderry line, its system comprised 114 route-miles.

The Strabane & Letterkenny linked the two Donegal narrow-gauge systems for the first time, since a siding connection was put in between the two adjacent stations at Letterkenny, and a link was also possible along the roads and quays between the two narrow-gauge termini in Londonderry. This made evident an embarrassing fact which hitherto nobody had noticed. All the narrow-gauge railways in Ireland shared the same 3ft gauge; but few of them, and not the Donegal and Lough Swilly, could interchange stock because nobody had thought to standardise buffer heights. The amount of through traffic exchanged at Letterkenny was always minimal, but what there was had to be worked coupled to special match-trucks with adjustable buffers and couplings, while mixed-gauge shunting on the Londonderry Harbour Commissioners' lines was fraught with peculiar extra difficulties.

The County Donegal had achieved peace with the world, despite being treated rather ungenerously by government after 1900, mainly by being able to shelter behind the skirts of its two protecting main-line companies after 1906. The Londonderry & Lough Swilly retained a suspicious independence as long as it could, still feeling that government had conned it into converting its gauge: but after the 1896 Act, passed largely for its special benefit, it agreed to accept a grant of £98,500 representing 80 per cent of the cost of an 18-mile extension from Buncrana to Carndonaugh, which it duly opened and operated from 1901. But it adamantly refused to have anything to do with the proposed Letterkenny & Burtonport Railway for a very long time; indeed the Irish Board of Works was ultimately forced to build and equip the whole 50-mile line itself, at a total cost of £319,000. This was very much the most expensive government-aided railway in all Ireland, and it is interesting to compare its cost with that of the broad gauge Galway to Clifden line, of the same length and through similar country, which cost only £274,000. Certainly the policy of favouring the development of narrow-gauge railways in Ireland had proved to be an expensive mistake. One trouble was that, while the Clifden line could be comfortably worked by elderly and semi-retired main-line locomotives and stock, to handle a similar volume of traffic on the narrow gauge the Lough Swilly needed new and relatively complex and expensive engines, of much the same weight and power as the depreciated broad-gauge ones. It was another consequence unlooked for in Westminster.

The Lough Swilly company agreed to work the Burtonport Extension when it was opened in 1903, but did so at first with such reluctance and half-heartedness that a scandal arose, and much high-level diplomacy was required to smooth ruffled feathers on both sides. Actually there was nothing wrong with the equipment which kept breaking down; the Lough Swilly people were just being

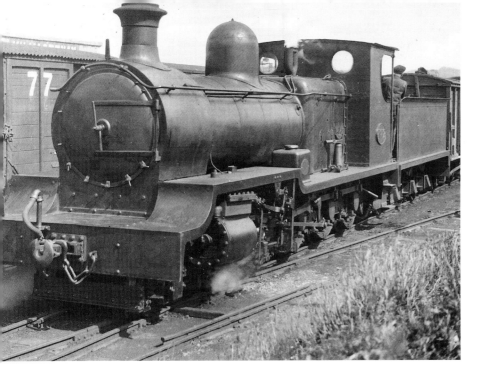

One of Ireland's only class of eight coupled tender engines, Londonderry & Lough Swilly Railway's No 12 on the 8.30am (mixed) Burtonport to Londonderry (Graving Dock) train at Kilmacrennan on 13 July 1931. This was one of a pair built by Hudswell Clarke & Co in 1905 (746/7) for working the heavy trains over the 74 miles from Londonderry to the western terminus. No 11 was scrapped in 1933 but No 12 remained complete until closure. A.W. Croughton

rather pig-headed about it. But, reforming in time, they got away with it once again.

The last new narrow-gauge railway to be established in Ireland, quite exceptionally as late as 1900, was the Cork, Blackrock & Passage. This had its origin in a 6½-mile broad-gauge line opened in 1850 from its own station (Albert Street) in Cork to Passage. It might perhaps be mentioned here that Cork was at this period unusual in that none of its railways were linked together. Only one of its five termini, Glanmire Road, had any connection with the rest of the Irish railway network. The two broad-gauge lines serving Capwell and Albert Quay stations, the Cork & Macroom and the

The railway station at Crosshaven, Cork, Blackrock & Passage Railway. Note that this was no tramway type system but a real railway complete with very adequate signalling, proper stations and a fast running commuter service. In the background is one of the line's 2–4–2 tanks about to run round its train. National Library, Dublin

Cork, Bandon & South Coast, were each for many years entirely isolated, although the broad-gauge Cork City Railway from 1910 linked Glanmire Road and Albert Quay through the streets. In 1925 the 24-mile Macroom line was diverted into Albert Quay by the reconstruction of its original route of 1866, which had been closed in 1879 when after some curious argument the C&M broke off all dealings with the CB&SC and severed its physical connection with it. So at least the broad-gauge lines were then linked.

The Cork & Muskerry narrow-gauge had its own tiny station at Western Road, remote from any other and although it co-existed with the trams came nowhere near any other railway at any point, and the Cork & Passage at the other end of town was in the same situation. When, therefore, they decided in the late 1890s to extend for 9½ miles to Monkstown and Crosshaven, they thought they might as well economise and adopt the 3ft gauge. They were dismayed, on going to London to seek funds for the project, that the pundits of Westminster had turned their backs on the narrow gauge, and they beat on all doors in vain until, down a mossy corridor, they found a gateway bound shut behind a festoon of spider's webs, and labelled 'Irish Board of Works' – the very body which had been set up by King William IV to lend money to deserving Irish public projects back in the 1830s, and which had been superseded (so everybody thought) by the new Act in 1883. Forcing an entrance, the C&P champions discovered a leprechaun sitting on a bag of gold, who gaily lent them £65,000 (which was never repaid). With this help they converted their old railway to 3ft gauge in 1900 and extended it as they desired in 1902 and 1904. And a very pretty railway it was too, as one would expect if fairy gold paid for it, even if it never carried any freight to speak of because it was isolated from the rest of the network. It even boasted the only length of double track on any Irish narrow-gauge line.

So by 1910 a degree of calm and order had been restored to the narrow-gauge railways of Ireland, and they had by and large settled down to do a generally useful job of work with no real financial problems, except in one or two localities, and no more than an entertaining minimum of scandals, financial or mechanical. But Ireland was then entering a period with no similar prospect of political peace, and the disturbances of the following decade had a dramatic effect on the whole of its railway network.

One railway which never survived the 'troubles' was the famous Listowel & Ballybunion, which closed permanently in 1924. As a monorail, it can hardly be described as a narrow-gauge line. It was built in 1888 without government assistance mainly as a showcase demonstration nine miles long of the practical possibilities of the Lartigue system. Unfortunately a sales pitch addressed to the world from one of the remoter corners of County Kerry suffered from a certain degree of inaudibility. But all the same the Ballybunion line, aided no doubt by its mere name, shines brightly in Irish railway legend and eclipses many more important railways which operated much more recently. The hand-operated double drawbridges which

were required at even the simplest level crossings, the turntable-points and strange shunting complexities, the footbridge-wagon marshalled in the middle of the train, and above all the problem of how to get one cow (or any odd number of cows) from one end of the line to the other (answer – borrow a couple of calves to balance it with), all go to illustrate the essential paradox of a railway which could only have been built in Ireland. If it had never existed, it would have been impossible to invent it.

*Listowel & Ballybunion Railway. The terminus at Ballybunion clearly showing the 'A frame' track, balanced locomotive and coaches and the complicated 'turntable' method of monorail track division. Note the general parsimony in the poor trackbed and corrugated iron railway buildings.* National Library, Dublin

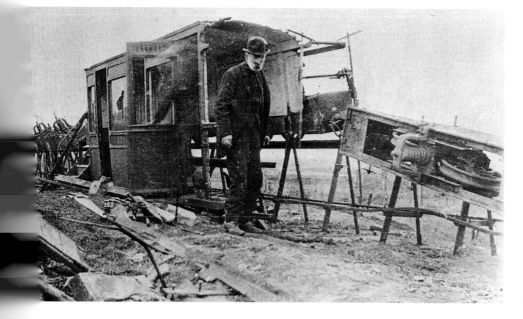

*Trouble on the Listowel & Ballybunion Railway; half the coach (the other side of the rail) has disappeared. However, this picture gives a good idea of how the stock was arranged and shows detail of a wheel and spring.* Millbrook House collection

Following the independence of the twenty-six counties in the southern part of the country, for which a separate government was established in 1922, all the many railway companies operating wholly within the area, whether broad gauge or narrow, were in 1925 amalgamated into the Great Southern Railways, and all the arrangements for local guarantees and subsidies were swept away. The GSR got firmly to grips with the situation and in a relatively short time all the narrow-gauge lines it had taken over, like all the broad-gauge routes, were overhauled and repaired and put into apple-pie order, as can he seen by almost any photograph. But the development of road transport began to change the picture fairly quickly, and even during the 1930s and in spite of the generally poor roads it became clear that the transport needs which most of the lines created after the 1883 Act had met would be served acceptably well and much more cheaply by buses and lorries. The GSR wasted no time or effort in modernising any of them to meet this threat; if they lost money with the old but well-maintained equipment they already had, they were candidates for closure. So the brief Indian summer when all the Irish 3ft gauge lines were in full operation and apparently prosperous came quite quickly to an end.

The first to go, not surprisingly, was the Cork, Blackrock & Passage, closed in 1932; in the following year the Cork & Muskerry, equally badly affected by bus competition, was also abandoned. The Tralee & Dingle lost its passenger trains in 1939, but rather in the manner of an ancient inebriate, reformed just before its liver finally ceased to function, hung to life for a surprisingly long time after that. Regular freight services ceased in 1947, but for another six years the line continued to operate, on a minimum-maintenance basis, enormous cattle trains once a month from the Dingle Cattle Fair. These too have passed into legend; rusty engines emerging from the ruins of Tralee shed, where the roof had collapsed onto them, to do battle once again with the Slieve Mish mountains, dubious viaducts which would only take one locomotive at a time, and double-headed trains getting across them, surprisingly good track on which extraordinary speeds had to be reached, to charge the next grade. There was the time when one engine's chimney fell off, but it *still* got to Dingle and back; and train crews setting off from Tralee knowing they would be on duty until they returned, even if that unpredictable event lay more than 24 hours ahead. There was never anything wilder in the other Wild West than the Tralee & Dingle, first and last and portrayed in the Prologue of this book.

That left among the lines wholly contained in the twenty-six counties, only the Cavan & Leitrim and the West Clare. The C&L in some ways lasted best. Right to the end it was an all-steam, well-maintained, fairly intensive operation with passenger as well as freight service. The GSR and its successor, the post-1945 CIE, thriftily drafted in the better locomotives from other narrow-gauge lines with compatible couplings, and refugees from the Cork,

*Castlegregory Junction, Tralee & Dingle section of the CIE in the summer of 1951 showing one of the empty cattle stock workings on its outward Friday journey. The engines are Hunslet built 2–6–0 tanks Nos 1T and 2T: they have just taken water at the tank on the right hand side of the photograph and are ready to tackle the formidable 1 in 31, 1 in 30 Glenagalt incline.* Ivo Peters

*Ireland's last roadside tramway, the Arigna branch of the CIE, originally part of the Cavan & Leitrim Railway. The whole line was kept open for the haulage of coal from Ireland's only commercial mines, and engines were imported from both the Cork, Blackrock & Passage and Tralee & Dingle sections. The Arigna branch was worked by three classes of engine, ex C&L 4–4–0 tanks, and two T&D varieties of 2–6–0 in No 4T (Kerr Stuart) and Nos 3T and 6T (Hunslet). The daily passenger train from and to Ballinamore, the railway's headquarters, was always mixed. Here on a wet day in August 1957 No 6T makes for home with one coach, a van and a string of coal wagons.*
P.B. Whitehouse

Blackrock & Passage and Tralee & Dingle came to inhabit the sheds and works at Ballinamore, never quite driving out all the original natives. Coal from Arigna kept the C&L busy, and even at the last minute this was increasing greatly in order to supply a new power station north of Dublin. But the end came, all the same, in 1959. The C&L, survived, but only briefly, the closure of its broad-gauge GNR connection at Belturbet.

For a while it seemed as if the West Clare would do better. It was fully dieselised in the early 1950s, with both railcars and locomotives, and offered better service than ever before. But it made no difference in the end; although it was the very last public narrow-gauge railway in any part of Ireland to survive, it still closed in 1961.

The fundamentally more prosperous narrow-gauge railways contained within the six counties that comprised Northern Ireland

*One of the last engines to be built for an Irish narrow-gauge line, the West Clare's No 7C (Hunslet Engine Co 1433/22 originally named* Malbay) *climbing out of Corofin station with the evening train for Kilrush during the summer of 1950.*
P.B. Whitehouse

*Ballycastle station in 1949 with a train composed of the two corridor coaches built for the Ballymena & Larne section and used to carry boat train passengers before the construction of the 5ft 3in gauge Greenisland loop. The engine is one of the two cylinder Von Borries 2–4–2 compounds built for the Ballymena line and transferred. The Ballycastle branch closed in 1950.*
P.B. Whitehouse

fared little better. The Castlederg and Victoria Bridge gave up in 1933; the Clogher Valley closed completely in 1941, despite the difficulties of wartime road transport. It had done rather well until then in carrying smuggled cattle since it followed the border for most of its length, but even in Ireland this was not enough to save it, nor had a partial dieselisation helped. The Ballymena, Cushendall & Red Bay had gone earlier, for passengers as early as 1930 and for freight in 1940 The connecting Ballymena & Larne lost its passenger services, including the boat expresses, in 1931, and was wholly gone by 1950. The Ballycastle, alone among the northern lines, had had a rather difficult time in the early 1920s, for the rather un-Irish reason that it went bankrupt. Not that it was uncommon to go bankrupt in Ireland, just that it was odd that mere bankruptcy forced it to close down for most of 1924, until the old independent company was sorted out and the railway taken over by the NCC. It became a spick-and-span little operation, like most of the southern lines (or more so) but the second thing the new nationalised Ulster Transport Authority did when it was formed in 1950 was to close it down. The first thing, of course, was to overhaul and repaint in new livery one of its locomotives. The two electric railways having already gone, that meant a clean sweep of all the narrow-gauge lines wholly contained within Northern Ireland.

The four railway companies which happened to cross the post-1922 border presented a more difficult problem. Neither government could sensibly reorganise them on its own, and neither would dream of doing anything in co-operation with the other, and so these four had to be left alone. The most important was the Great Northern, certainly far and away the best railway in Ireland, which remained in great varnished Edwardian splendour for many years, (with the addition of a few diesel railcars, with which it attempted to

*In 1928 the Northern Counties Committee (the LMS in Ireland) built five special coaches at their Belfast works. These were centre corridor vestibuled vehicles with lavatory accommodation for use on the boat trains over the Larne Harbour to Ballymena section and were the last word in narrow-gauge coach design; two of the coaches were composites, two others had brake compartments. In the event they were only in use for three years as the opening of the Greenisland loop gave faster 5ft 3in gauge connections to Belfast. Later the coaches went to the Ballycastle section and on closure (in 1950) were purchased by the County Donegal Railways Joint Committee. As LMS NCC No 318 a full third rebuilt on a B&L underframe stands at Larne in September 1932. The design is reminiscent of early LMS standard gauge vestibule vehicles in England. R.G. Jarvis*

*Londonderry & Lough Swilly Railway. One of the five compartment slatted seat six-wheel third class coaches in Pennyburn yard, Derry, 1952. These vehicles, dating from the end of the last century were in use on Buncrana excursions to the end, mixed in with later Burtonport Extension bogies. P.B. Whitehouse*

show what it could do if only it could raise funds). Then in 1957 the Ulster government unilaterally closed down its half of all the GNR cross-border lines except the Dublin to Belfast main line, leaving the southerners little choice but to follow. The same dastardly act put paid to the other cross-border broad gauge, the splendidly piratical Sligo, Leitrim & Northern Counties, which as late as 1949 had obtained two new locomotives by simply ordering them, cash on delivery, only to tell the makers when they were delivered 'sorry we've got no cash'. The most cursory enquiry at the time the order was placed would have confirmed that. The world market for new 5ft 3in gauge 0-6-4Ts being undetectable, there was little the makers could do about it, and for a few last years the SL&NC had new, if not modern, power for its trains.

The other two cross-border railway operators were our old friends the County Donegal and the Londonderry & Lough Swilly; from the 1920s their histories, so alike originally, followed quite different paths. The Lough Swilly, like the GSR, kept its railway to

# L. & L. S. RLY.

# TIME TABLE

### Operative on MONDAY, 27th SEPTEMBER, 1937, and thereafter until further notice.

| Down Trains. | | Week Days. | | | | | Up Trains. | | Week Days. | | | |
|---|---|---|---|---|---|---|---|---|---|---|---|---|
| | | A.M. | P.M. | P.M. | | | | | A.M. | P.M. | P.M. | P.M. |
| **LONDONDERRY** | dep. | 10 0 | | | | | **BURTONPORT** | dep. | 8 30 | 2 0 | 4 15 | |
| Gallagh Road | - | A | | | | | Dungloe Road | - | 8 36 | 2 6 | 4 21 | |
| Bridge End | arr. | 10 11 | | | | | Kincasslagh Road | - | 8 41 | 2 12 | 4 27 | |
| | dep, | 10 25 | | | | | Crolly | - | 8 56 | 2 29 | 4 44 | |
| Burnfoot | - | 10 30 | | | | | **GWEEDORE** | arr. | 9 6 | 2 39 | 4 54 | |
| **TOOBAN JUNC.** | arr. | 10 33 | | | | | | dep. | 9 15 | 2 44 | 4 59 | |
| Inch Road | - | | | | | | Cashelnagore | - | 9 35 | 3 2 | 5 17 | |
| Fahan | - | | | | | | Falcarragh | - | 9 46 | 3 12 | 5 27 | |
| Lisfannon Golf Links | - | | | | | | Dunfanaghy Road | - | 10 15 | 3 38 | 5 54 | |
| **BUNCRANA** | arr. | | | | | | **CREESLOUGH** | arr. | 10 20 | 3 43 | 5 59 | |
| **TOOBAN JUNC.** | dep. | 10 40 | | | | | | dep. | 10 25 | 3 48 | 6 4 | |
| Carrowen | - | 10 49 | | | | | Barnes Halt | - | A | A | A | |
| Newtoncunningham | - | 11 5 | | | | | Kilmacrenan | - | 10 55 | 4 20 | 6 36 | |
| Sallybrook | - | 11 21 | | | | | Churchhill | - | 11 5 | 4 30 | 6 46 | |
| Manorcunningham | - | 11 27 | | | | | Foxhall | - | 11 16 | 4 41 | 6 57 | |
| Pluck | - | 11 35 | | | | | New Mills | - | A | A | A | |
| **LETTERKENNY** | arr. | 11 50 | | | | | Oldtown | - | 11 35 | 4 55 | 7 11 | |
| | dep | 12 20 | 5 50 | | | | **LETTERKENNY** | arr. | 11 40 | 4 58 | 7 14 | |
| Oldtown | - | 12 24 | 5 54 | | | | | dep. | 12 0 | | | |
| New Mills | - | A | A | | | | Pluck | - | 12 13 | | | |
| Foxhall | - | 12 42 | 6 12 | | | | Manorcunningham | - | 12 20 | | | |
| Churchhill | - | 12 52 | 6 22 | | | | Sallybrook | - | 12 27 | | | |
| Kilmacrenan | - | 1 10 | 6 39 | | | | Newtoncunningham | - | 12 45 | | | |
| Barnes Halt | - | A | A | | | | Carrowen | - | 12 55 | | | |
| **CREESLOUGH** | arr. | 1 35 | 7 1 | | | | **BUNCRANA** | dep. | | | | |
| | dep. | 1 40 | 7 7 | | | | Lisfannon Golf Links | - | | | | |
| Dunfanaghy Road | - | 1 44 | 7 12 | | | | Fahan | - | | | | |
| Falcarragh | - | 2 12 | 7 40 | | | | Inch Road | - | | | | |
| Cashelnagore | - | 2 25 | 7 55 | | | | **TOOBAN JUNC.** | arr. | 1 5 | | | |
| **GWEEDORE** | arr. | 2 43 | 8 10 | | | | | dep. | 1 10 | | | |
| | dep. | 2 55 | 8 18 | | | | Burnfoot | - | A | | | |
| Crolly | - | 3 4 | 8 29 | | | | Bridge End | arr. | 1 18 | | | |
| Kincasslagh Road | - | 3 22 | 8 47 | | | | | dep. | 1 23 | | | |
| Dungloe Road | - | 3 30 | 8 55 | | | | Gallagh Road | - | A | | | |
| **BURTONPORT** | arr. | 3 35 | 9 0 | | | | **LONDONDERRY** | arr. | 1 35 | | | |

*Note in Up Trains P.M. column:* Dungloe and Falcarragh Fair Days excepted, 4th and last Thursday of each Month.

*Note in Up Trains P.M. column:* Dungloe and Falcarragh Fair Days only.

"A" Stops to pick up passengers if required; also to set down passengers on notice being given to Guard at previous stop.

N.B.—See separate Timetable for full particulars of the Company's Omnibus Services.

**JAS. WHYTE, Manager & Secretary.**

*Londonderry & Lough Swilly Railway wagon stock at Londonderry (Graving Dock) in 1950. Note the fact that those supplied to the Burtonport Extension were always separately lettered as the bogie van (one of three only). The van No 45 is one of a total of 29 with a centre canvas cover.*
P.B. Whitehouse

*Londonderry & Lough Swilly Railway, Pennyburn shed and station, Londonderry, in the early 1930s.* A.W. Croughton

*One of the ex Derwent Valley (the English standard-gauge concern at York) railcars as CDRJC No 3 at Donegal on 15 July 1931. This had been purchased by the DVLR as a Ford lorry chassis and fitted with a sister vehicle to run back to back, using one of the motors at a time. They were both purchased by Forbes of the CDRJC for £480. At Castlefinn the Free State customs officer lay in wait and in spite of protests obtained a 33⅓% duty claiming that they were motor buses. The vehicles were converted to the narrow gauge by the Great Northern Railway (Ireland) at its works at Dundalk.*
A.W. Croughton

the bitter end in splendid apple-pie order; it also boasted the four most powerful locomotives in all Ireland – another Irish oddity of course that these, two 4–8–0s and two 4–8–4Ts, should be narrow gauge. But as early as 1929, its Ulster suspiciousness of all governments returning, it had decided that its only possible commercial future lay in moving the whole of its business across to road transport, and slowly and deliberately it did just that. The Buncrana–Carndonagh line was closed successfully in 1935; an attempt was made to close the Burtonport Extension in 1939 that was rather less successful in that demolition was halted by riots, and then the war forced a resumption of freight service over most of the line, as far as Gweedore, mainly to carry turf for fuel, which lasted until 1947. Reduced to its original Buncrana and Letterkenny operation, and freight-only after 1948, the Lough Swilly kept running trains, still smartly and with gleaming engines, until 1953 when the remainder closed and the whole system, which had covered 99½ route-miles at its peak, ceased to exist. But the company was still in business, and indeed remains so to this day, running buses and road haulage in the district it has always served.

Accepting that its railway was doomed spared the Lough Swilly the effort of trying to modernise or reform it. The County Donegal fought hard, on the other hand, mainly in the direction of using diesel railcars to provide a more frequent, and faster passenger service than was possible with steam traction, at a much lower operating cost. From the early 1930s on, it had a considerable fleet of

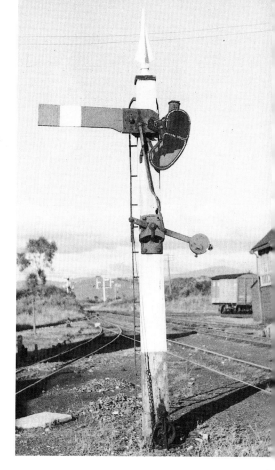

*The up starting signal at Donegal station showing distinct signs of Midland parentage. On the right is the signalbox controlling the entrance and exit to the east with the three arm bracket signal clearly shown to the left of the post; to its left is the advance starter whilst the Ballyshannon branch comes in from the right. P.B. Whitehouse*

*Castlefinn was the customs examination point for County Donegal trains in the Republic of Ireland (the line crossed into the Six Counties just beyond Clady, the border being the River Finn) and vans were sealed here. The accompanying photograph shows CDRJC 4–6–4 tank Erne with a Strabane-bound mixed at Castlefinn station along with the customs officer. P.B. Whitehouse*

*Make do and mend; carriage repairs at the Stranorlar headquarters of the County Donegal Railways Joint Committee in 1957. During these years of mortal decline the coaches saw little service part from holiday specials and use as brake vehicles (carrying passengers on the quiet) on the rear of regular freights.*
P.B. Whitehouse

railcars, all of some character but all basically buses on wheels. They never spent money on diesel locomotives, but instead sensibly kept the best of the steam locomotives to run separate freight services and extra summer holiday excursion trains; with this policy it seemed for some time to be succeeding. One blow was the UTA closure of the Londonderry line in 1954, which until then had remained a CDJR-worked all-steam operation; but the killer was the gradual deterioration of the track, and above all certain steel-girdered bridges, which finally caused a deliberate government decision to close the whole system totally in 1959. This proved that in the long term running trains economically is not enough; if you let the civil engineering maintenance get into arrears any railway becomes very difficult to save. The Donegal was survived, for some months, by the totally unmodernised Cavan & Lietrim, and a couple of years by the wholly modernised and highly-maintained West Clare, which possibly proved something else.

So ended the public narrow-gauge railways of Ireland, of which not a sleeper or a rail remains. Just as most of them had been brought into existence, so they were mostly wiped out by the whims of government policy. All were lines of great character, even if their larger eccentricities were mostly exaggerated. Neither in their operating patterns, nor their equipment, did they have very much in common with narrow-gauge lines in Britain; rather, they resembled those of France, Spain or Italy.

116

# CHAPTER FIVE
# LOCOMOTIVE DEVELOPMENT

The first narrow-gauge locomotives used in Britain were employed on private railways owned by industrial or mining companies, and a number have already been listed. One could argue even that the very earliest locomotives of all were narrow gauge, though only just. Trevithick's Penydarren engine, the first application of steam power to rail traction after his Coalbrookdale example of 1803, ran on a tramroad of 4ft 2in gauge, and the machines built by Matthew Murray for the Middleton Railway at Leeds in 1812, the first commercially successful and permanent use of locomotives on any railway, were built to 4ft gauge. One might also notice that the first two locomotives of the Padarn Railway, built for it in 1848 on its relocation and reconstruction, by the otherwise little-known firm of Horlock in South London, were also of 4ft gauge. They were quite extraordinary 0–4–0s of immensely long 10ft wheelbase, with a wheel at each corner and dramatically inclined cylinders well behind the front axle. Although they were superseded as long ago as the mid-1880s, one of them still exists, and is one of the dozen or so extremely early locomotives preserved in Britain; it is well worth a pilgrimage to the Penrhyn Castle Museum in North Wales to see it.

When the Festiniog Railway began to contemplate applying steam locomotives to the business of a *public* narrow-gauge line, it was going into relatively uncharted territory and hesitated long between differing schools of thought about their design. In some ways the situation was a re-run of the arguments for and against the broad gauge of the Great Western which had raged 25 years earlier, when one widely-felt cause of alarm was that as the wheels of a locomotive were placed closer together, so the likelihood of its falling over sideways on curves was increased. Contemplating wheels only 2ft apart, the low-centre-of-gravity fetishists had a field day, though nobody seems to have started a scare about a Festiniog locomotive being overturned by a sharp gust of wind. Finally the firm of George England, at the Hatcham Ironworks (again in South London) was given the order for the first four. They set the boilers as low as possible, without regard for convenient access to the inside valve gear, or for adequate or indeed any ashpans. By adopting the once fairly common but by the 1860s already obsolete practice of stopping the main frames short just behind the second axle and ahead of the firebox, they avoided the need to raise the boiler sufficiently to get the frame plates beneath the grate, at the cost of having to hang the cab and the drawbar on the back of the firebox.

*Two of the Festiniog Railway's first steam locomotives originally named* The Princess *(1863) and* Palmerston *(1864) (left of picture, behind) at the upper terminus of the line, Duffws, probably in the early 1870s.*
Millbrook House collection

Otherwise the England 0–4–0s were entirely conventional engines, just rather small ones. Delivered by horse and cart from the main line railhead at Caernarvon during 1863, they proved themselves in service fairly quickly, though some modifications were needed. Domes had to be added to the boilers to reduce priming, and the side tanks extended upwards into saddle tanks to increase the water capacity; both these changes raised the centre of gravity quite markedly, but experience soon showed that this did not matter a bit. The small tenders provided did not carry water at all but only coal. Two more rather larger but basically similar engines followed from the same builder in 1867.

Two more public narrow-gauge railways adopted steam traction during the 1860s, the Talyllyn and the Festiniog & Blaenau. The 2ft 3in gauge Talyllyn went to the then well-known firm of Fletcher, Jennings in Whitehaven, which produced two designs for it. The first locomotive, later named *Talyllyn*, started as a short-wheelbase 0–4–0 saddle tank with both axles ahead of the firebox, very like the Festiniog engines but more strongly built with a conventional full-length frame. Despite following this precedent, the engine in this form was unsatisfactory, pitching nose- and tail-down very badly, possibly because Fletcher, Jennings had used volute springs, more flexible than the laminated springs of the England engines. *Talyllyn* had to be modified at once by the addition of a trailing pair of carrying wheels, converting her into an 0–4–2T, in which form she gave good service and indeed still continues to run, though the lash-up nature of the modification always gave trouble as the rear axle had no sideplay. To avoid all these problems, the second locomotive, *Dolgoch*, became an 0–4–0T with the second axle behind the firebox, thus obtaining a long wheelbase of 6ft 6in. Since it was

118

considered important to keep the valve gear between the frames, it had to be driven off the leading axle in a complex and unconventional way carefully patented by Mr Fletcher, which furrowed the brows of several generations of fitters at Towyn. But it served; indeed it was not until 86 years later, possibly a world record, that any train was drawn on Talyllyn metals by any locomotive other than one of this very early pair.

The Festiniog & Blaenau in 1868 obtained two 0–4–2Ts from the firm of Manning, Wardle, whose designer had obviously studied *Talyllyn* in its modified form. These engines were evidently successful as they worked the whole traffic of the F&B until its gauge was converted in 1883, when they were scrapped. They might have been offered first to the Festiniog, but by then that line had outgrown them. It had adopted steam power because growing traffic had threatened to overwhelm it so long as it continued to depend on horses and gravity; but traffic continued to grow and after a few years the six little England 0–4–0s were in danger of being overwhelmed in turn.

Something much more powerful was needed. One could of course build more 0–4–0s and simply double-head the trains, but there was something absurd in that idea, with two men already on

*One of the larger Festiniog Railway 0–4–0 saddle tanks in its final form. Welsh Pony (built George England 1867 and rebuilt FR Boston Lodge 1915) in the yard at Blaenau Festiniog in the early 1930s. The engine was taken out of service in 1938 pending reboilering and has not run since F. G. Carrier. Millbrook House collection*

119

*Locomotive working was not introduced on the 4ft 0in gauge Padarn Railway immediately upon opening but* Fire Queen *along with sister* Jenny Lind *were certainly the first two engines to be used from 1849. The two locomotives worked all the traffic until they became time expired in the 1880s.* Jenny Lind *was scrapped but* Fire Queen *is now on view in the Penrhyn Castle Industrial Museum.* Penrhyn Castle Industrial Railway Museum and D. Rendell

each tiny machine. The sharp curves and restricted clearances of the Festiniog ruled out any idea of extra length (on a rigid wheel-base), or extra height and width, within which a more powerful engine could be designed. The only solution was to take up the new idea put forward by Robert Fairlie, of carrying a much larger boiler on two bogies to give sufficient flexibility for the curves, with one or both of those bogies powered with independent cylinders and motion, fed through flexible steampipes, or more accurately at that time, pipes with moveable ball-and-socket joints.

The practical difficulties of the scheme were considerable; indeed it was almost 100 years before the expensive, complex and hard to maintain jointed pipes could be replaced with truly flexible pipes of new materials. But this awkwardness was well worth tolerating for the immense improvement in economical haulage capacity. George England delivered the first Fairlie locomotive *Little Wonder*, to the

120

Festiniog in 1869. It was under-designed, awkward to maintain, and racked itself to pieces in short order, finally having to be withdrawn and scrapped in 1882. But during that time it had become world-famous as it demonstrated its great tractive capabilities, more than those of two 0–4–0s combined, before delegations of engineers from many parts of the world.

So before the end of the 1860s the typical pattern of Welsh narrow-gauge locomotive development had been set and it has remained between those parameters ever since. The great majority of engines were small and simple machines, running on only two or three axles, without much sophistication and relatively limited in size and power. Most lines in fact remained content to use engines of this sort exclusively. But there was a small number of much more advanced and powerful engines, running on four or five axles, used by the few lines which due to train weights or steep gradients needed something radically better.

During the 1870s the pattern was confirmed. The Festiniog had built for it three more Fairlies, two of the classic type with two steam bogies and double boiler, chimney at each end and twin central fireboxes, and one of the less common Single Fairlies, with a conventional boiler and only one power bogie, the other end being supported by a small-wheeled carrying bogie. Thus an 0–4–4 Single Fairlie looked very much like a conventional 0–4–4T rigid-frame engine. The difference, that the driving wheels were articulated and able to swing round on the curves, gave a more smooth-riding and adhesive machine at the cost of increased maintenance expense, but hardly showed on the outside. Two more Single Fairlies, 0–6–4Ts this time, were built for the North Wales Narrow Gauge Railway, which also had a rigid-frame 0–6–4T for comparative purposes. The other new locomotives of the decade were all small; three 0–4–0Ts, soon enough rebuilt as 0–4–2Ts, for the Corris Railway, and no fewer than 10 vertical-boilered and primitive 0–4–0s by the Caernarvon firm of de Winton for the Penrhyn Railway on its

*The Festiniog Railway single Fairlie 0–4–4 tank* Taliesin *at Boston Lodge works. Built in 1876 by the Vulcan Foundry this engine was similar in many respects to those built for the North Wales Narrow Gauge Railway. It proved to be the fastest and most economical engine on the line. The Company refused to sanction a new boiler and it was withdrawn in the early 1930s (boiler scrapped 1935). However, all is not lost, as construction work is now under way on a replacement locomotive to this design using the latest technology and materials. Festiniog Railway Company*

conversion to steam propulsion, seven for use in the quarry itself and three rather larger ones for the main line. In fact a considerable number of these odd locomotives were built by de Winton for various lines and quarries in North Wales, and crude as they were a few lasted into the 1950s. The ill-fated Gorseddau Railway's only locomotive was one, which cannot have helped matters much.

During the 1880s and 1890s, with the exception of one final Double Fairlie for the Festiniog, all new locomotives built for the Welsh lines were quite small. The Penrhyn and Padarn lines each had ten more 0–4–0Ts, three of the former fairly large to replace the de Wintons on the line haul, and all the others relatively tiny and mostly cabless machines for quarry work. The Padarn also acquired three new 4ft gauge 0–6–0Ts of good solid conventional design to replace their ancient and eccentric 0–4–0s. The Hafan & Talybont acquired its ill-fated super de Winton, a percolator to outperk all others but not much use at pulling trains, and its one 2–4–0T, while the Glyn Valley had its first two 0–4–2Ts with boxed-in tram-engine bodies. The only other new engines of these two decades were the five original Swiss-built rack engines for the Snowdon line, one of which as we have seen soon came to a sad end. It was not until after 1900 that any larger locomotives were built for any Welsh narrow-gauge line.

However, when they came, they were quite impressive. The first two were a pair of 2–6–2Ts for the Vale of Rheidol; admittedly they had the advantage that the Rheidol had no clearance problems and rather easier curves than the Festiniog, so it was not too difficult to design a conventional non-articulated engine weighing 25 tons, heavier by three tons than the final Festiniog Double Fairlies, simpler to maintain and nearly as powerful. But the older machines scored since their full weight was available for adhesion, while the Rheidol tanks with their non-driven axles carrying some of the load, bore only 17 tons on their driving wheels. For all their awkwardness and complexity, the Fairlies were considerably the better train-pullers in adverse conditions, approximating after all to a modern diesel or electric in their layout. One oddity of the two Rheidol 2–6–2Ts of 1902 was that they were built by the firm of Davies & Metcalfe, better known for their injectors and vacuum brake equipment, and were in fact the only two locomotives ever built by them.

The same year saw the construction of the two 0–6–0Ts of the Welshpool & Llanfair Railway, by Beyer Peacock. At 19 tons these were large engines only by Welsh narrow-gauge standards, and they would have been dwarfed by many running on the same 2ft 6in gauge in other countries. Indeed, considering the frightful grades of the W&L, with long sustained lengths of 1 in 30 in each direction, they were certainly rather undersized and would have been in trouble had traffic been any heavier than it was.

The North Wales Narrow Gauge Railway acquired two new and relatively large engines a few years later. Their original rigid-framed 0–6–4T *Beddgelert* was worn out by 1906 and had to be withdrawn, a fact which says something about the share of the work it must have

*Beyer Peacock of Manchester built three 0–4–2 tramway type engines for the 2ft 4½in gauge Glyn Valley Tramway; No 3* Glyn *(3500/92) is seen here at Glynceiriog in the late 1920s. The railway closed entirely in July 1935 and all locomotives were cut up for scrap. The name-plate* Glyn *is preserved in the Narrow Gauge Railway Museum at Tywyn. A.W. Croughton*

*Snowdon Mountain Railway is the only steam rack railway in the British Isles. The rack system used is the Abt and all locomotives were built by the Schweizerische Lokomotiv und Maschinenfabrik company of Winterthur, between 1895 and 1923. No 2* Enid, *seen here at Llanberis in 1954, is the oldest extant (SLM 924/95), No 1* Ladas *having been destroyed in an accident before the opening.* P.B. Whitehouse

*Davies & Metcalfe of Romiley built a pair of 2–6–2 tanks for the Vale of Rheidol Railway in 1902; their resemblance to the Manning, Wardle 2–6–2 tanks recently acquired by the Lynton & Barnstaple Railway was noticeable to say the least. Works Nos were 1 and 2. After acquisition of the line by the GWR in 1923 the locomotives were renumbered 1212 and 1213. Old No 1 was withdrawn in 1932 (cut up 1935); No 2 (1213) was rebuilt to correspond with the Swindon 1923 engines Nos 7 and 8, and now runs as No 9, carrying the name* Prince of Wales. A.W. Croughton

One of the smaller terrace locomotives built by the Hunslet Engine Co, Leeds for the Dinorwic Quarry adjacent to Llanberis. The engine (822/03) is Maid Marian, *now preserved. Similar locomotives were built for the Penrhyn Railway at Bethesda. The gauge was a nominal 2ft 0in (actually 2ft 10¾in).*
K. Cooper

performed since 1878 compared with the two Single Fairlies. It was replaced by a 2–6–2T, a somewhat smaller redesign by Hunslet of the Rheidol engines, differing from them by having the more conventional and modern feature outside valve gear. It was named *Russell* after the railway company's Receiver, and he must have deserved the honour, to have been able to find the money for the investment after the NWNG had been bankrupt for many years. Two years later, oddly enough, another new engine was acquired; this time it was a modernised and rather handsome Hunslet version of a Single Fairlie 0–6–4T, named *Gowrie*. This engine has always been a mystery. On paper it should have been a very useful machine, yet it was sold in 1918 for war work and did not long survive. Some say that its being sold proves it must have been a poor tool, but the NWNG was in a bad way by 1918, freight-only, run-down and at death's door, so the alternative theory that they were driven to sell their best engine simply to raise more cash also carries conviction. We shall never know the truth of it now.

All the other new engines of the period leading up to 1914 were small. The Glyn Valley bought another 0–4–2T; the Padarn and Penrhyn another half-dozen 0–4–0T quarry engines each. For the Penrhyn these were the last new steam locomotives; thereafter second-hand machines were purchased instead.

Indeed, second-hand locomotives became common currency

125

*GWR 822* The Earl, *one of the two Beyer Peacock Welshpool & Llanfair Railway 0–6–0 tanks (3496–7/02) at Llanfair Caereinion in the late 1920s. The name plate has been moved to the cab side and the original number-plate (No 1) previously on the cab side removed. The name of the other locomotive* The Countess *had to be shortened to* Countess *to fit the cab side. A.W. Croughton*

*The last engine to be purchased by the North Wales Narrow Gauge Railway (in anticipation of the completion of the line to Portmadoc) was* Gowrie, *an 0–6–4 single Fairlie (Hunslet 979/08). The engine was sold into Government service in 1918. The photograph was taken at Dinas Junction in 1909. G.M. Perkins; W.A. Camwell collection*

after the First World War for one very good reason; each side built behind its static lines of trenches in France a very considerable network of 2ft or 60cm gauge light railways to bring supplies up to the front, and great numbers of locomotives as well as all sorts of rolling stock were mass-produced to work them. After 1918 these machines, some of which were still brand-new, came onto the second-hand market, and several varieties were brought back for use on narrow-gauge railways in England and Wales. The commonest of these was the 4–6–0T designed and built by Baldwin of Philadelphia, to the specifications of the British War Office - who in turn were quoting the details of a type designed for the job earlier by Hunslet of Leeds, who were unable to supply them in the enormous numbers needed. Few of the Hunslet 4–6–0Ts returned to Britain, though some found work elsewhere, as far afield as South America, and it was not until 40 years later that one example of the

alternative and superior 2–6–2T designed to the same specification by the American Locomotive Company was put to successful use in this country.

The Baldwin 4–6–0T was a quite powerful but rough and ready and by no means lovely engine. Only two worked in Wales; the financially hamstrung Welsh Highland, successor to the North Wales Narrow Gauge, scraped together the pennies to buy one to replace *Gowrie*, and though little loved by any of the crews who banged and jolted along on it, who were always complaining of its awkwardnesses and bad habits, it does seem to have been the most consistently reliable of all that unfortunate railway's modest fleet of engines, working steadily throughout its short life. Indeed for one whole year it was the only locomotive that actually worked. The Glyn Valley Tramway had another, and spent a great deal of money not only on converting its gauge to 2ft 4½in, but on improving the quality of its fittings and equipment, culminating in providing it with a handsome copper–capped chimney. The Penrhyn Railway purchased three of the Alco 2–6–2Ts but failed to make anything of them and sooner than keep trying quickly sold them again for scrap (though one ended up happily enough in Australia).

The other War Department contribution was internal combustion. Steam locomotives behind the lines had been at a disadvantage because the clouds of smoke and steam they produced often drew

*Not only did the Glyn Valley Railway purchase one of the 2ft 0in gauge (nominal) ex War Department Baldwin 4–6–0 tanks, it (after converting it to the 2ft 4½in gauge) considerably improved the engine's appearance by fitting it with a copper capped chimney and lining out the paintwork. This was the only non tramway type engine on the line. As Glyn Valley No 4 it stands at Chirk on 31 May 1934, just over a year before closure of the whole line on 6 July 1935. Passenger services ceased on 6 April 1933. H.C. Casserley*

artillery fire. It therefore became important to design a smokeless locomotive, and this gave the first great boost to petrol or diesel traction on many railways in the world. The Simplex company of Bedford in England, and the Baldwin works in the USA, each came up with a standard type of 40hp four-wheeled locomotive weighing about eight tons, with about the tractive capacity of a steamer of the same weight. Each used a very large, slow-turning, four-cylinder petrol engine as prime mover, with a friction clutch and gearbox akin to motor-car practice, though arranged for equal speeds in each direction. The Simplex however had the gearbox within the wheelbase, and the drive taken to both axles by chains, while the Baldwin had a much larger gearbox mounted at one end and drive transmitted to the wheels by jackshaft and side rods. The Simplex had a central cab with a generally dome-shaped body conveniently made of armour plate, which was of some advantage in France, while the Baldwin had a steam locomotive type cab at the opposite extremity to the gearbox. Many Simplex locomotives were brought back for a variety of industrial lines in Britain, and were found to be so successful that the company continued to build them, in all gauges and various sizes, shorn of armour plate but sometimes acquiring decadences like self-starters, for almost another 40 years. The Festiniog acquired one of each type for shunting; the other Welsh lines held back from anything so adventurous and stayed faithful to steam, though the Welsh Highland made it pretty plain that if only it could afford some it would prefer to use them exclusively. It did experiment in 1929 with a diesel built by Kerr Stuart, which proved successful enough. Though Kerr Stuart's bankruptcy prevented a sale on terms WHR could accept. The only other internal-combustion locomotive was a fairly successful petrol-engined four-wheeler on the 4ft gauge Padarn which ran for a while in the 1930s.

There were several other post-1918 acquisitions. The Corris in 1921 purchased one of the standard Kerr Stuart contractors' 0–4–2Ts of the *Tattoo* class, the smallest but one of the range, with some extras like vacuum brake and steam heat; apart from its odd 2ft 3in gauge, the Corris curves would have been too sharp for the Alcos or Baldwins. The Snowdon, during the brief postwar boom, acquired three more rack engines from Switzerland, of greater power than its earlier machines. The Padarn had built three more small 0–4–0Ts for quarry work. The most impressive new engines, however, were certainly a pair for the Vale of Rheidol, built by the Great Western Railway at Swindon in 1923.

The Rheidol, as a neglected limb of the Cambrian, had passed to the GWR in the 1922–3 amalgamations, and the GWR took it rather to heart. The existing stock, two 2–6–2Ts and a 2–4–0T, was felt to be inadequate, and taking the original Davies & Metcalfe design as a starting point and using as many standard parts as possible (including cylinder castings from steam railcars) Swindon came up with a solid, chunky, and improved 2–6–2T weighing 25 tons, by some way the heaviest, though not as we have seen the most

powerful, narrow-gauge steam locomotives ever to work in Wales (until lately). One of the originals was taken back to Swindon and rebuilt to conform, the 2–4–0T was cut up, and in 1925 a splendid high-frequency timetable was operated during the holiday season, with trains flashing up and down the valley like a commuter service, several booked non-stop. Unhappily they were not very well filled, so things cooled down again in subsequent years. The other original 2–6–2T, after some years at Swindon awaiting a decision about rebuilding, was scrapped instead, and the Rheidol became the three-engine railway it has since remained. For many years, while the two later locomotives were numbered 7 and 8, the surviving original was No 1213 which fitted nicely in the list among the other ex-Welsh-minor-company engines taken over by the GWR but looked odd in a line-up at Aberystwyth. It was not until 1949 that 1213 was renumbered 9. With the exception of one final quarry 0–4–0T built for the Padarn/Dinorwic system in 1931, the Rheidol tanks were the last new locomotives built for any Welsh narrow-gauge railway until modern times.

The locomotives used on the 3ft and wider narrow-gauge lines in England were in general terms rather like those on the majority of Welsh 2ft lines – small and simple. Oddly enough, the engines used on the English (and Scottish) lines of less than 3ft gauge tended to be larger and more powerful than most of their Welsh equivalents.

Developments started in the 1870s with the three 3ft gauge systems, Isle of Man, Ravenglass & Eskdale, and Southwold. As we have already noticed, the Isle of Man locomotive story is extremely simple; as they began, so they carried on. The first three small Beyer, Peacock 2–4–0Ts of 1873 were simply repeated with minor modifications by the same builder until the last was delivered in 1926, by which time there were no fewer than 15. Admittedly they got slightly bigger with each order, but even the final example was still a relatively small machine, weighing only 23¼ tons against the 19 tons of the originals. The solitary exception was the one and only 0–6–0T, built by Dübs for the Manx Northern's mineral traffic.

The Southwold started in 1879 with three even smaller 2–4–0Ts, by Sharp, Stewart; but in its consistently parsimonious manner, finding quite soon that two machines were sufficient to handle the business, it returned No 1 to the manufacturers, and only in 1893 did it increase its fleet by ordering another machine, this time an almost equally tiny but rather more serviceable 2–4–2T, which from then on seems to have done a lion's share of the work. The railway's suicide may have been triggered off by the fact that this engine needed shopping in 1929; certainly it was cut up at that time, while the others lingered unliquidated until 1942. In 1914, most uncharacteristically, the company went wild and purchased a considerably larger (though still fairly small) Manning, Wardle 0–6–2T, quite a handsome and purposeful-looking machine. Reverting to character,

*Isle of Man Railway 2–4–0 tank No 2 Derby (Beyer Peacock 1254/73) at Douglas in the 1920s. This was one of the first batch of three engines taking their names from the Duke of Sutherland (1) Lord Derby (2) and John Pender MP (3).* A.W. Croughton

they then seem to have used it very seldom, judging by the few surviving photographs.

The old Ravenglass & Eskdale was another two-engine railway, or latterly somewhat less than that. Manning, Wardle supplied in 1875 and 1876 a pair of quite tiny 0–6–0Ts, weighing about 15 tons and even smaller than the early Isle of Man 2–4–0Ts; they survived until the demise of the 3ft gauge line, although one of them was unusable after about 1908.

And so things remained for 20 years or so, until the first of the 2ft gauge railways was opened. The 2–4–0T was definitely the preferred type during this period; the Isle of Man kept on buying them for three more decades; the 3ft 6in Jersey Railway finally had five, and the Rye & Camber two, one tiny and one smaller still. It was not until the Lynton & Barnstaple opened for business in 1898 with three Manning, Wardle 2–6–2Ts that things got more interesting. These machines were definitely impressive, and at over 27 tons quite the biggest 2ft gauge locomotives ever to operate in Britain, while bigger than any of the 3ft gauge engines outside Ireland. What is more, they were clearly the models from which the later Vale of Rheidol engines were taken, though quite superior in many details; Davies & Metcalfe took a long step back, for example, in preferring to use inside valve gear even while they copied the basic outside-frame layout. The Swindon rebuild, and later new construction, for the Vale of Rheidol, did no more than put matters

*The only 0–6–0 tank on the Isle of Man, No 15* Caledonia *was built for the Manx Northern Railway (Dübs 2178/85). After amalgamation it was little used, spending most of its time at the rear of the locomotive shed. It was fitted with a snow plough and occasionally used in the winter for snow clearing.*
K. Cooper

131

right, but even the Swindon engines would probably not have been a match for the Lynton & Barnstaple machines.

Finding that three engines were not sufficient, and needing a fourth in a great hurry, the Lynton & Barnstaple in 1898 obtained one from Baldwin of Philadelphia. Several British and Irish mainline railways bought locomotives from Baldwin about this time, and all the history books say it was because they were needed in a great hurry and English manufacturers could not deliver in time. The story somehow lacks conviction. More likely, Baldwin was interested in expanding its sales and the British railway companies were getting restive at the treatment they were getting from their traditional suppliers; it would be interesting to know the truth. Anyhow, for whatever reason, the L&B joined the party. Its purchase was a rather aggressively American-looking 2–4–2T, weighing 22 tons and so very large and powerful for its wheel arrangement, particularly as most of its other dimensions were only slightly smaller than the Manning, Wardle Locomotives, and in one important matter considerably larger. The English engines had water tanks of rather modest size, only 550 gallons. Davies & Metcalfe at least got one thing right in increasing this figure to 584 gallons on the Rheidol examples; Baldwin sensibly increased it still more on its 2–4–2T to 665 gallons, which must have made the Devon enginemen a great deal happier. This one fact would be enough to explain why the American machine evidently became a firm favourite on the L&B. When the Southern took over, they added a fifth locomotive, a

*Southern Railway, Lynton & Barnstaple Railway section. Manning, Wardle & Co, Leeds, 2–6–2 tanks at Pilton shed Barnstaple on Sunday 29 September 1935 waiting to take the last public train. On the left is No 188* Lew *(actually ordered by the Southern in 1925 and the only engine to be sold without being broken up) and No 759* Yeo *of 1896.* Lew *was shipped to Brazil in 1936 and has never been traced since.* Donovan E.H. Box; Millbrook House collection

the coal-mine railway that had operated on part of the site previously. Later locomotives obtained by other lines were either second-hand or repeats (with or without added details) of earlier designs; the very last were the Lynton & Barnstaple 2–6–2T of 1924 and Isle of Man 2–4–0T of 1926.

'Second hand' here means 'ex-military'. The Baldwin 4–6–0Ts built for the War Department have already been mentioned in connection with the Welsh Highland and Glyn Valley lines, which had one each. The Ashover, starting from scratch in 1925, had no fewer than six, all basic and unmodified. As things wound down and the original impressively frequent passenger service dwindled to a shadow and vanished, the locomotives swirled untraceably about like autumn mists, undergoing processes of mating, amalgamation and cannibalisation so that although on paper four survived to the end in 1951, management would have been hard put to it finally to produce more than two complete examples if the auditors had ever chosen to inspect them. But except for a few Simplex machines around Clay Cross, the Ashover remained faithful to the type.

The other railway making use of secondhand war surplus locomotives was the Sand Hutton, following its conversion to 18in gauge in 1921. Sir Robert Walker acquired three Hunslet 0–4–0Ts from a temporary line in a meat storage depot at Deptford, although they were practically identical to some engines that had run on the much larger system nearby at Woolwich Arsenal, and give or take the difference between the well tanks of the Sand Hutton engines

*The last wholly new British (not Irish) locomotives designed for a public narrow-gauge railway (except for Southwold's orphan 0–6–2 tank) were two Andrew Barclay 2ft 3in gauge 0–6–2 tanks for the Campbeltown & Machrihanish Railway, delivered in 1906 and 1907. A.W. Croughton*

135

*Ex War Department Baldwin-built 4–6–0 tank* Peggy *at the head of a passenger train on the Ashover Light Railway. The engines were named after the children and daughter-in-law of the Chairman of the Clay Cross company. The engines were shipped from France to England in pieces, thus there is some doubt as to the actual works number.* Peggy *was presumed to be Baldwin 44743/17. The engine was taken out of stock and cut up in 1950. A nameplate is in the possession of one of the authors and on exhibition at the Narrow Gauge Railway Museum, Tywyn.*
A.W. Croughton

*Whilst most industrial concerns linking themselves with the main line naturally set up their private standard-gauge railways to link with the main lines, the quarry companies with their larger independent systems made considerable use of the narrow gauge. The variety of locomotives in use was enormous, as can be seen by the examples shown here, all from the Midlands.*

*The French tank is a Veuve Corpet L. Louvet 0–6–0 of 1903. This metre gauge engine carrying the name* Nantes *came to England with its sister* Cambrai *in 1934. Both ended their working lives at Waltham Quarries, Leics, in the late 1950s.* Nantes *was broken up in December 1960 but* Cambrai *is preserved at the Narrow Gauge Railway Museum at Tywyn adjacent to the Wharf station of the Talyllyn Railway.* K. Cooper

*Jee's Hartshill Quarries Nuneaton, 0–6–0 tank* Stafford *(Bagnall WB1911/1912) 2ft 6in gauge, photograph on 25 October 1952.* K. Cooper

and the side tanks used later, not unlike the last surviving Woolwich Arsenal steam locomotive now running on the Bicton Gardens railway in Devon. As we have seen, they did the Sand Hutton very well during its decade of operation. When the end came, the last Sand Hutton driver, who had been devotedly maintaining them more or less on his own, was shown how to use an oxy-acetylene blowtorch and told to cut them up.

When we come to consider the locomotives of the Irish narrow-gauge railways, we are faced with quite a different situation. The first lines and earliest engines were much in line with British parallels, generally modest in size, duty, and specification. But when political encouragement began to be applied to the development of the Irish narrow gauge, things changed. Certainly the greater distances and larger volumes of traffic that had to be contemplated meant that it was necessary to use more powerful machines, although some of the first political railways did try to make do with small types, usually with unsatisfactory results. But the lack of planning, forethought, or standardisation which was induced by the ill-considered legislation brought about a degree of confusion on the mechanical side which quite matched the financial and administrative disorganization. We have already noticed that, even in matters so basic as settling the height of the combined central buffer and coupling (which was *itself* more or less universal), little was achieved and the common track gauge concealed an enormous variety of incompatibilities. Dr J. Prideaux has calculated that, of the total of 144 steam locomotives built for the Irish 3ft-gauge lines, there were no fewer than 66 different designs using 20 different wheel arrangements. No 'class' of locomotive achieved double figures; the most

137

*Worsdell von Borries 2–4–2 compound tanks were built for the Belfast & Northern Counties Railway and later the Midland (NCC) by Beyer Peacock. The locomotive shown here, No 101, was constructed in March 1909, 16 years after the original class members and was built at York Road works. Sister locomotive No 102 worked for a time between Ballymoney and Ballycastle but its later years were spent running to and from the paper mills between Larne and Ballyclare. Renumbered to 41 in 1939 the locomotive saw service on the Ballycastle line until closure in 1950. However, it was not withdrawn until 1954.*
R.G. Jarvis

numerous type in fact were the eight 4–4–0Ts built for the Cavan & Leitrim. On paper the next most numerous were the six compound 2–4–2Ts built for the Belfast & Northern Counties; but since they were turned out at various dates between 1892 and 1920, and one of them was rebuilt as a 2–4–4T, even this group shared features more on paper than in practice. Most engines were built in ones and twos and threes. A steady flow of profitable business no doubt resulted for many years between the principal builders in Leeds and Glasgow and the remoter corners of Ireland, which helped to make life pleasant and interesting for all concerned except the Irish ratepayers who ultimately, in most cases, paid.

It all presents a confused picture of development which is difficult to summarise consistently, and any general survey can only be a broad-brush one with many exceptions. Instead of following the chronology strictly, it seems best to divide the railways into those which more nearly followed the British pattern, and those which at first or later became more ambitious.

The first few lines, in Ulster, followed British precedents most closely. While narrow gauge, they were quite solidly built with their own rights-of-way, not following the public roads, and were in no sense tramways. The Ballymena pair of lines, to Cushendall & Red Bay and to Larne, started off in the 1870s with three 0–4–2Ts and two Beyer Peacock 2–4–0Ts respectively, the latter duplicates of the Isle of Man engines. Three 0–6–0Ts were added soon after, and despite the heavy gradients they sufficed for a number of years. Some larger 2–4–2T two-cylinder compounds, weighing 35 tons, were introduced in 1892 (the type which eventually numbered six!),

partly to handle the developing passenger business between Larne and Ballymena, linking the cross-channel ferry from Stranraer with Londonderry, and saving 16 miles in comparison with the all-broad-gauge route from Larne to Ballymena via Greenisland. Some of the smaller locomotives were saddle tanks, always fairly unusual to find in passenger service, but apart from this they were all reasonably conventional and serviceable machines, of small to medium size.

The Ballycastle Railway started business in 1880 with three small 24-ton 0–6–0Ts, saddle tanks again, which sufficed until the early years of the new century, when they acquired from Kitson two quite large and advanced 4–4–2Ts, weighing 39 tons. Following the NCC takeover in 1924 the 0–6–0Ts were replaced by some Ballymena 2–4–2Ts, made surplus by declining traffic on the older system. There was thereafter a degree of interchangeability between the two lines, which makes keeping track of their equipment a little difficult, though since Ulster is still in Ireland each line's original engines actually ended their days on the other. The Ballycastle had some large bogie passenger coaches seating 80 in its independent days; following the end of passenger service on the Ballymena lines in 1931, the very fine and still new Midland looking corridor open compartment stock built only a few years earlier for the boat trains was transferred to Ballycastle, making that railway quite the best-equipped of all Irish narrow-gauge lines so far as passenger stock was concerned. Three of these ex-Larne coaches went after 1951 to the County Donegal, and so survived until practically the end of narrow-gauge passenger working in Ireland.

The next group of lines also followed British precedent to some extent, but had different roots there. In fact all could be classed as steam tramways, since they followed the public road to a greater or lesser extent, the Castlederg & Victoria Bridge and Clogher Valley

*In 1931 compound 2–4–2 tank No 110 was rebuilt into a 2–4–4 tank (with a Midland Railway Class B boiler as used on Class 2F 0–6–0s) at the York Road works of the NCC in Belfast. This sadly proved a failure, the engine proving too rigid for the curves. It was withdrawn in 1946. R.G. Jarvis*

lines in particular for most of their lengths. This brought them into a complex situation. As we have seen, the Westminster legislature in its wisdom decided that steam locomotives working along or beside the highway, in order to avoid accidents caused by bolting horses and frightened livestock, had to be disguised so that they could not be recognised as steam locomotives This generally meant casing them in a box-like body like a van or a coach, while the driving wheels and motion, which might have given the game away, were also concealed behind platework, thus sparing the beasts from being confused and maddened by the complex of revolving and recipro-cating pins, rods, and other parts. Awed by this masterly analysis of animal psychology from the corridors of Westminster, railways and locomotive builders did at first very much what they were told to do in the matter, even in Ireland. Experience soon showed that while there was some minor advantage to be gained from having the loco-motive crew mounted on the front of their engine as they proceeded along the road, since they had a better view of chickens, dogs, and small children disappearing under their wheels and so were better placed to do something about it, if so minded, there was little evidence to support the proposition that horses or cows could tell any difference between a locomotive that was disguised as a box and one that was not, still less the difference between those fitted with inside Stephenson and outside Walschaerts valve gear. Indeed, the behaviour of a cow meeting a train in the streets of Balleygawley or Ballydehob was the same as the behaviour of one next to a Scotch express flying through the meadows of Staffs or Northants behind a substantial fence – initial panic, followed soon enough by boredom

*One of the two Ballycastle locomotives as rebuilt by the NCC in 1926/7 and renumbered 113. They were intended for use on the Ballymena & Larne line though No 113 returned to the Ballycastle section for a short while during the Second World War. Note the standard NCC type chimney, cut down boiler mountings and cab – necessary if the engines were to clear the Ballymena & Larne bridges. The engines were originally built by Kitson in 1908.* R.G. Jarvis

as familiarity bred contempt, and the frightful apparition was observed to take no interest either. So one common feature of this group of lines was that they soon found that box bodies and double cabs were rather a waste of time. The good visibility advantage could be obtained easily enough by having an ordinary tank engine and always running it cab-first. Some lines, including the Cavan & Leitrim, had locomotives that were capable of having a second cab built on at the smokebox end, but never actually had them fitted and instead turned the machines round so that they always ran bunker- or cab-first. Eventually the rule was relaxed, particularly after Irish independence, and second cabs and skirting round the wheels were discarded also. The accident rate remained about the same.

Apart from the strange tram-engine syndrome, and the roadside or even road-centre location of the track, this second group of lines tended to be more lightly built, with steeper gradients and less powerful, indeed often insufficiently powerful, locomotives. The Castlederg & Victoria Bridge was first, opening in 1884 with a pair of 18-ton 0–4–0T tram engines. A third was added a few years later, but no real success was achieved until two considerably larger machines, a 2–6–0T and an 0–4–4T, weighing around 26 tons, were obtained later.

The other four lines of this group were all opened more or less simultaneously, in 1886/7; the Clogher Valley, the Schull & Skibbereen, the Cork & Muskerry, and the Arigna branch of the Cavan & Leitrim. The Tralee & Dingle followed in 1891, but thereafter roadside locations for steam railways were dropped; experience showed that the accident and nuisance rate was too high to compensate for the relatively small saving in first cost.

Of these lines, the Schull & Skibbereen certainly had the worst experience; its three 15-ton 0–4–0T tram engines were not only too feeble to cope with the line's grades but they were burdened with an unsuccessful experimental boiler design. Within a couple of years these machines had failed so utterly that the line had to be closed down to await the arrival of a much more powerful, but still quite small, 24-ton 4–4–0T. Two more of these followed as funds were raised, in 1905 and 1914, and finally during the 1920s the last of the 0–4–0Ts was retired, though admittedly they had been rebuilt and improved for the re-opening.

The Clogher Valley, a much longer and busier line but with rather better grades, opened for business with six 24-ton 0–4–2T semi-tram engines, encased but with one cab only, normally run cab-first, plus a similar but larger and more powerful 0–4–4T; these sufficed throughout the line's existence, although after the Castlederg & Victoria Bridge closed the Clogher Valley acquired the latter's 2–6–0T, rebuilding it as a 2–6–2T of very odd appearance, with all the wheels bunched together closely in the middle. The Cork & Muskerry, for a time one of the most successful and prosperous of all the Irish narrow-gauges, paid no heed to the tram-engine fetish in spite of its substantial length of road-centre track in

141

*Schull & Skibbereen Railway 0–4–0 tank No 2 (originally named* Ida*) at Skibbereen on 29 May 1924, the last year of the line's independence. Though extensively rebuilt it was one of the first three locomotives constructed for the railway by Dick, Kerr & Co, Kilmarnock, in 1886. It was the last survivor of the original tram engines and was scrapped in 1925 when taken over by the Great Southern Railways.* A.W. Croughton

Cork. It had a mixed fleet of conventional engines, three 2–4–0Ts, three 4–4–0Ts, an 0–4–2T, and in 1893 a pair of 0–4–4Ts. None of these machines made any more concession to other road users than having substantial cow-catchers fitted, even normally running chimney-first. All the other lines in this group incidentally also used cowcatchers, otherwise rare in British and Irish practice.

The Cavan & Leitrim was a hybrid, with a main line from Belturbet to Dromod which had no tramway features and was substantially built, and a roadside tramway branch from Ballinamore to Arigna that was very tram-like indeed. Since the railway was in Ireland, it naturally turned out that the greatest volume of heavy traffic originated at Arigna. The original locomo-

*Working cab first, steam tramway fashion, Clogher Valley Railway's 0–4–2 tank No 6* Erne *(complete with side skirts) heads the 10.45am mixed train to Maguiresbridge at Tynan the Eastern terminus on 13 July 1935. The platform adjoined the Great Northern (Ireland) line to Belfast while the western terminus connected with the same railway's branch to Enniskillen.*
A.W. Croughton

*When the assets of the Castlederg & Victoria Bridge Tramway were auctioned on closure in 1934 one of the locomotives, 2–6–0 side tank (Hudswell Clarke & Co 698/04), was acquired by a Belfast contractor who exchanged it for Clogher Valley Railway No 7 which required a new boiler. The latter company rebuilt it in 1936 where it ran as No 4 and was chiefly used on fair days at Ballygawley and Fivemiletown when traffic was particularly heavy. When the railway closed the engine was purchased by the Turf Board of Eire. A.W. Croughton*

*Ballinamore station on the Cavan & Leitrim Railway showing 4–4–0 tank No 8* Queen Victoria *on a Dromod bound train during the last year of independence, 17 May 1924. This was one of the first eight locomotives built for the railway by Robert Stephenson & Co (2619/84). As built they were fitted with stovepipe chimneys.*
A.W. Croughton

tive fleet consisted mainly of the mass-production batch of eight 4–4–0Ts that we have already noticed, relatively large for their wheel arrangement at 27 tons, plus one much bigger machine, a 37-ton 0–6–4T of entirely different design. All these engines were designed to be capable of working both the 'main line' and the Arigna branch, on which they normally ran cab-first in the early days; this apart, they had no tram-engine features, though as has been noted the 4–4–0Ts could have had front cabs added relatively easily if government had ever insisted on it.

The Tralee & Dingle was another hybrid line, at least in a kind of way. It followed a roadside location practically throughout its length, though generally on a reserved strip on one side of the highway, so from the civil engineering point of view it could have been classified as a tramway with no argument. Its locomotives, however, were akin to those of the Cavan & Leitrim, with tram-engine appurtenances added but only one (0–4–2T No 4) actually ran thus. On the other hand, they went to a different builder, Hunslet, who looked at the problem in a different way, and the T&D opened for business in 1891 with three 2–6–0Ts for the main line and one 0–4–2T intended for the Castlegregory branch – a very inadequately sized fleet, though not too badly outclassed as to power and general suitability. A 2–6–2T also by Hunslet was added in 1892, a very similar machine to the 2–6–0Ts but its slightly larger coal and water capacity necessitated the extra pair of wheels. In 1895 another 2–6–0T was obtained, and in 1902 and 1903 two more, though from a different builder (Kerr Stuart). In spite of this restlessness they were very similar to the earlier machines; in fact, the Tralee & Dingle had a more uniform and characteristic fleet of locomotives than any other Irish narrow-gauge line except one, particularly after the tramway-styled 0–4–2T met an early end in 1907. Whether this unusual uniformity was because the Dingle management was wisely satisfied with a sound basic design of machine, or whether it was because the line was so remote, and its financial condition so notoriously rocky, that no carpet-bagging locomotive builder's traveller ever thought it worth while journeying to Tralee to solicit an order, is now one of those never-to-be-answered questions, though the early Dingle management did not show much evidence of good sense in other directions.

The last group of Irish narrow-gauge lines were the thorough-breds, fully-equipped and substantially-built main lines, intended to handle heavy traffic. They were built to the 3ft gauge maybe for political reasons, but certainly not for sound engineering ones though nothing was skimped. The two principal railways in this class were the Londonderry & Lough Swilly, and the County Donegal. But the West Clare belonged to it as well, and so in its own small way did the Cork, Blackrock, & Passage, although as we have seen it adopted the narrow gauge at a later date and for rather different reasons. Its locomotive history as a narrow-gauge line was very simple and can be cleared out of the way first. It had only four engines, all identical 2–4–2Ts by Neilson Reid built in 1899 and

*Tralee & Dingle No 1, a Hunslet 2–6–0 tank of 1889 rests inside Tralee shed on 5 August 1953. It was one of three 2–6–0 tanks constructed for the opening of the line, with protective skirts over the wheels. Board of Trade regulations were relaxed soon after opening of the railway and the skirts were removed.* K. Cooper

*Three of the four Neilson, Reid & Co, Glasgow, 2–4–2 tanks built for the Cork, Blackrock & Passage Railway in 1899 at Cork in GSR days, 10 June 1932. The engines are Nos 6, 5 and 7 respectively (NR&Co 5563/2/4). All four were transferred to the Cavan & Leitrim section on closure in 1932. These engines worked a very smartly timed service during the heyday of the CB&P Railway.* H.C. Casserley

weighing a fairly moderate 37 tons only. But they were excellent machines, with larger driving wheels than any others on the Irish narrow gauge (4ft 6in diameter), able to run smoothly and sweetly at speeds of 50mph and more. They were certainly in a class of their own.

One of the many things the Donegal and the Swilly lines had in common, even if the list did not include compatible couplings, was a relatively large and complex fleet of steam locomotives, numbering 21 and 18 respectively, making these two concerns the largest by this measure as well as by route-mileage (114 and 99).

The Donegal started its narrow-gauge operation in 1889 with three little 20-ton 2–4–0Ts, but soon grew out of these and between 1893 and 1900 took delivery of six 30-ton 4–6–0Ts of much greater capacity. Even these were soon enough outclassed. In 1900 were delivered two engines with the unusual wheel arrangement of 4–4–4T, weighing in at 38 tons, primarily intended for working on the easier grades of the original Finn Valley section from Strabane to Stranorlar, though they were also later found on the Strabane–Londonderry line, which the Donegal always worked even though officially it belonged to the NCC. There followed four even larger engines, 4–6–4Ts weighing 44 tons and built in 1904. Nor was this all, for at various dates between then and 1912 no fewer than eight 2–6–4Ts were built for the line, though they were of two slightly different types, and weighed either 43 or 50 tons. The second type had superheaters and piston valves – the first really modern engines on any Irish narrow gauge, though by the same token not by any means the cheapest to produce.

*One of the two 4–4–4 tanks built by Neilson Reid & Co, for the County Donegal Railways Joint Committee, No 11* Hercules *(6104/02) the only design with this wheel arrangement on an Irish railway. The photograph was taken at Stranorlar shortly before withdrawal in 1937.*
A.W. Croughton

146

The Lough Swilly followed a similar path, and indeed some of its locomotive types resembled their Donegal equivalents pretty closely. They started with a number of 2–4–0, 0–6–0, and 0–6–2 tanks of no special interest, although the latter were mildly unusual in having well-tanks, and were pretty to look at but had very limited water capacity. The Donegal look-alikes were four 30-ton 4–6–0Ts; thereafter the Swilly followed a different design path, with eight substantial 4–6–2Ts of 40 and 42 tons. These were followed by certainly the four most remarkable narrow-gauge locomotives in Ireland, two 4–8–0 tender engines built in 1910, and two closely-related 4–8–4 tanks built in 1912. The latter were certainly the heaviest and most powerful narrow-gauge locomotives in Ireland or the British Isles at 51 tons, though with tenders included the 4–8–0s weighed 58tons. But apart from that, they were also the most powerful locomotives on any Irish railway at the time they were built. By most measures of output—tractive effort, grate area, and so on— they were considerably more powerful than the largest County Donegal locomotives and the relatively small extra weight reflected the fact that they had been designed to keep weight down. But none was built with or later provided with superheaters. Even though it had rather shorter distances to run, the Swilly in its great days had a heavier traffic to handle than the Donegal, and at any rate on the Burtonport extension worse grades, and it needed this

*One of the early Londonderry & Lough Swilly engines No 4* Innishowen, *an 0–6–0 tank by Black, Hawthorn & Co (834/85). Its coupling rods were removed from the first pair of wheels after trials but in later years they were replaced and an overall cab fitted. The engine's name was removed in 1928 and it was scrapped in 1940 after being laid by for some years.* L&GRP

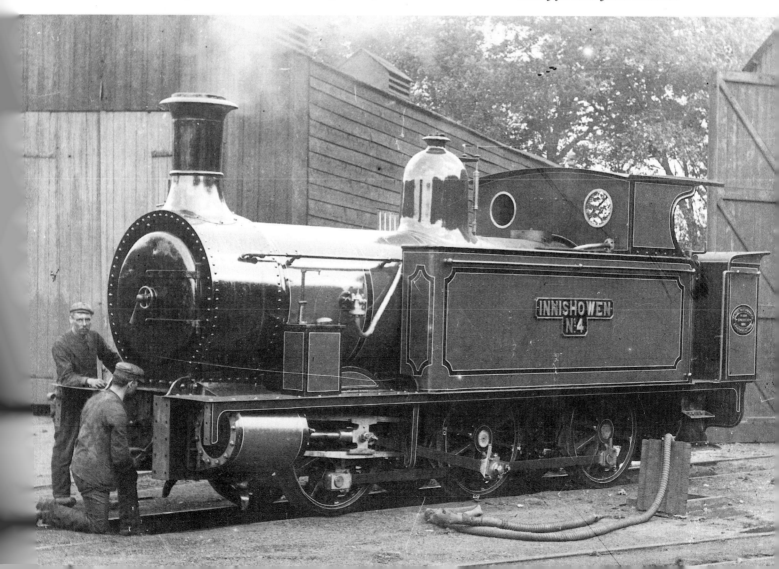

*In September 1921 Hudswell Clarke delivered the last two engines of the Londonderry & Lough Swilly Railway stock, the only 4–8–4 tanks in the British Isles. Both engines survived until closure. This engine, No 5, was used on the demolition train in 1953. Both were offered for sale in running order, but in those days no museum wanted them and they were cut up for scrap in 1954. This photograph was taken at Londonderry in August 1930. H.C. Casserley*

*George Hopkins (ex Midland Great Western Railway) introduced this neat class of 0–6–2 tanks to the West Clare Railway. Built by Dübs & Co in 1892; each carried a name. Technically the locomotives were built for the South Clare Railway but were used indiscriminately over the whole system. No 5C stands at Ennis in 1932. H.C. Casserley*

extra power even if it characteristically kept clear of modernisms.

The West Clare began in 1887 with three fair-sized 0–6–0Ts, and soon acquired three more rather larger 0–6–2Ts; these last were rather odd-looking since the trailing wheels were the same diameter as the driving wheels. There was also something a little odd about the appearance of their next locomotives, four 36-ton 2–6–2Ts, perhaps the oversized and very long water tanks, though the length of the railway they had to work gave every excuse for these. The best-looking West Clare locomotives were certainly the last, five 4–6–0Ts by Kerr Stuart, slightly larger than but closely akin to the Scottish-built engines of the same wheel arrangement on the Donegal lines. The final two of the West Clare engines, built in 1922, were the last new steam locomotives for any Irish narrow-gauge lines. They had outside valve gear, not otherwise a universal feature of the better Irish locomotives, though the final Donegal and Swilly engines had it and an odd assortment of others, including

most of the Dingle machines.

One belief quite widely held by narrow-gauge locomotive designers was that outside frames were an advantage when it came to laying out the more powerful types, particularly since they gave smoother riding. Experience abroad showed this theory to he complete moonshine, but it was certainly held by the Irish lines; all the larger Donegal, Swilly, and West Clare engines had outside frames, and a fair random selection of others also. In fact an outside-frame locomotive probably rode worse, other things being equal, since the layout forced the cylinders further apart and made balancing piston thrusts and reciprocating masses much more difficult. There were perhaps some minor advantages in accessibility for maintenance.

Once closures started, still-usable locomotives from one railway were often transferred to another to run out their mileage. Occasionally the newcomer flourished well enough on its new territory to survive longer, and be put through shops alongside or even in preference to the originals. There was a degree of interchangeability between the Ballymena and Ballycastle lines from early days, reinforced when the former lost its passenger services not long after the latter was taken over by the NCC from the former independent company, and most of the better survivors migrated northward. One Cork & Muskerry 0–4–4T was rescued from the debris in 1934

*The West Clare 4–6–0 tanks were introduced by W.J. Carter, but to the design of William Barrington, the consulting engineer to the railway. They came from varying manufacturers from 1903 onwards. No 1 Kilrush was a Hunslet engine (1098/12) and is seen here in lined out West Clare livery at Ennis in 1924. The number plate reads WCR, 1, 1912. A.W. Croughton*

149

*CIE 0–4–4 tank No 6S was originally a Cork & Muskerry (6K) engine; built by Thos Green & Sons (200/93) it was transferred to Skibbereen in 1938 but did little work. After the line closed it was left (as seen here in 1950) outside the shed until Inchicore claimed it for scrap.* P.B. Whitehouse

and sent to the Schull & Skibbereen; much more powerful than the natives, it was little loved and did not long remain, except as derelict. On the other hand, all four 2–4–2Ts from the Cork, Blackrock & Passage survived its closure in 1932 by being transferred to the Cavan & Leitrim, where they prospered. They were too heavy and long-wheelbased for the Arigna branch, but by the same token were more at home on the 'main line'. They lasted well at Ballinamore, though not quite to the bitter end.

The hardiest migrants were certainly the Tralee & Dingle engines, following cessation of all services except the monthly cattle train in 1947. Three, including the 2–6–2T, went to the Cavan & Leitrim, where they survived until final closure in 1959; two more went to the West Clare in 1953, leaving only three, or arguably two-and-a-half since No 2 had declined to the original T&D state of being barely self-motivating, to see the end at Tralee.

Only a few Irish narrow-gauge lines ever supplemented steam power with modern traction. The Tralee & Dingle built a four-wheeled inspection car in 1922 which remained in service, latterly on the West Clare, until 1960, though it never seems to have seen public use. The West Clare toyed with a pair of four-wheeled rail-cars during the 1930s, without much success. The Castlederg & Victoria Bridge had a similar vehicle.

Only three lines made a determined effort with internal-combustion power, and far and away the most successful was the County Donegal. It had its first petrol-engined inspection car as early as 1907, most of them more or less obvious bus-conversions. In 1931

150

it took delivery of its first diesel-engined railcars, and from then until 1952, when the last pair were delivered, a cumulative total of no fewer than 20 railcars took over almost all the regular passenger services and, having the capacity to haul one or two wagons as well, a great deal of the freight particularly at the remoter ends of the line. Oddly enough one firm, Walker Brothers of Wigan, had an effective monopoly of all Irish narrow-gauge diesel construction after the mid-1930s.

The early Donegal railcars were bus-shaped four-wheelers, needing to be turned at each end of the run since they could not operate (except when shunting) in reverse. In the case of the Ballyshannon to Strabane through service, they also needed to be turned in the middle of the run since the junction at Donegal town faced the wrong way; this was done with passengers on board. The first diesel cars had a leading radial truck added to try and smooth out the riding on curves; very soon the design settled down to an articulated type, with cab and engine on a leading four-wheeled unit, generally with its wheels coupled with rods, while the coach body formed an articulated trailer, supported at the far end on its own bogie. The typical Walker unit was occasionally found away from the Irish narrow gauge; the Great Northern of Ireland had a few, and (perhaps influenced by the common broad gauge) the Victorian Railways in Australia ordered a large fleet of them in the early 1950s, including a variant with a central powered unit and articulated trailers fore and aft. Some things they all had in common, on whatever gauge: they were reliable, cheap to operate, fast, and pretty rough to ride in. Roaring along in one on the

*Ballinamore shed, Cavan & Leitrim section CIE, in August 1957, with ex Tralee & Dingle 2–6–0 tank No 3T being coaled. Note the extremely poor quality of the coal, used in the main as power station fuel.*
P.B. Whitehouse

*Two of the CDRJC diesel railcars at Killybegs terminus in 1958. The leading vehicle, No 14, is typical of the mid 1930s design – its diesel traction portions powered by Gardner 6L2 engines while its body was constructed at the Dundalk works of the Great Northern Railway. Note the half cab which was replaced in Nos 15 onwards with a more fashionable full cab. No 14 ran 896,044 miles during its years of service.* P.B. Whitehouse

*The Clogher Valley railway came into the diesel railcar business in 1932 purchasing the vehicle from Walker Bros. With a Gardner 6L2 engine it was the first articulated power car to run in Ireland. On closure in 1942 it was purchased by the County Donegal Railways Joint Committee where it served until closure in December 1959. It ran 348,977 miles on that system, was used for the demolition work and now rests in the Belfast Transport Museum.* A.W. Croughton

Donegal in its latter, declining, days, was quite an experience.

Two other lines followed suit. The Clogher Valley in the 1930s acquired one Walker railcar, plus a power unit arranged to run on its own like a one-ended locomotive; both were successful in cutting costs and speeding up the service, but could not transform the basically unhappy economics of the line and hardly postponed its closure. Much the same could be said of the much later dieselisation of the West Clare. Four Walker railcars took over the passenger service there in 1952, doubling the one-train-a-day frequency and setting some interesting speed records on this, like all CIE passenger lines, very well-maintained track. Three Walker-built diesel locomotives, twin-bogie, twin-engined, centre-cab variations on the railcar theme, took over the freight in 1955. Closure still took place in 1961; the totally unmodernised, 100 per cent steam-worked Cavan & Leitrim had gone only 21 months earlier.

Except in the case of the Donegal, where perhaps it gave the railway another 10 years, diesel traction never postponed closure, a general statement, incidentally, with wider application than just the Irish narrow-gauge railways. The economies it produced in operation were, of course, impressive; but railways operators are too often inclined to take a loco-centric view of the universe, and locomotive operation is only one part of a railway's trading. If the enterprise is failing anyhow, the reduction in costs can be unimportant compared with the frightful capital investment required. From this point of view, dieselising the West Clare was an aberration, coming as late as the 1950s, but the Donegal acted when there still seemed a sporting chance of success. And in doing so it did, after all, set an example followed eventually by the main line systems on both sides of the Irish Sea. Experiments with diesel power by the narrow-gauge lines of England and Wales were very small-scale and rather timid.

The true narrow-gauge railway in Ireland is dead except for the turf-bog lines of the Bord Na Mona, which are of course industrial railways. However a short section of the old Tralee and Dingle line has been rebuilt at Tralee as an important local tourist attraction and the 3ft gauge has also returned to Londonderry, where tracks have been laid over the ex-GNR broad-gauge line from Londonderry Foyle Road towards the Donegal border. This line, the Foyle Valley Railway will be able to recreate something of the County Donegal with the restored railcar No 12 and 2–6–4 tank No 6 *Columbkille*.

In Wales, and in England, on the other hand, narrow-gauge railways still survive in a relatively big way. None any longer have much transport function, with an exception in the case of the Dymchurch to New Romney school train on the RH&DR, simply going to prove the rule that tourism and entertainment is the name of the game for the survivors. But there is nothing strikingly new about this; such traffic was an important part of the estimates for several lines in the latter part of the 19th century, as we have seen. This book is not intended to cover modern developments on the lines still running in

the 'preservation era'; but all the same, note should be taken of the fact that narrow-gauge locomotive development has restarted, in a small way. Certain lines – the Welshpool & Llanfair perhaps the most notable example – have imported steam locomotives to suit their gauge from far afield, some of them more modern than any built for British use, which were practically all in any case pre-1918. Interestingly enough, one of the Alco 2–6–2Ts from First World War service has been acquired from France and put to work successfully on the Festiniog. Several more railways have actually built new steam locomotives, notably including two new Double Fairlies on the Festiniog, a prime example of revival of an antique design for what must surely have been antiquarian and sentimental reasons, although admittedly some advantages were taken of modern technology in a few small ways. Even leaving aside diesel traction, a modern steam design would surely have served the FR better. But then, with 'preservation' as a motive, museum-curators' thinking creeps in, and designs and methods have to be justified not on their merits but on their historical antecedents. There is much to enjoy and approve of in the modern approach to the narrow gauge in Britain, but in that regard at least the great pioneers of the past would surely find our thinking uncomfortably restrictive. And certainly, the only railway that can truly be said to be 'preserved' is one that has finally ceased to run trains.

Opposite:
*Still resembling the earlier days a Festiniog train stands at Tanybwlch in April 1969. The locomotive is a double Fairlie No 3* Earl of Merioneth *(originally named* Livingston Thompson *and numbered 11 but almost at once renumbered 3 vice* Mountaineer*). It inherited the single Fairlie name* Taliesin *in 1932 and was christened* Earl of Merioneth *by the new management in 1961. Both* Merddin Emrys *and* Livingston Thompson *were built at Boston Lodge Works, in itself a great tribute to the engineering prowess of the Festiniog Railway. No 10 was completed in 1879 and No 3 (as No 11) in 1885.* C.M. Whitehouse

*The first new Fairlie built for nearly 70 years: the Festiniog's* Earl of Merioneth *Mark II, which entered service on 19 July 1979, replacing the 1885-built engine which had carried the same name, now retained as a static exhibit.* N.F. Gurley

# APPENDIX

## TABULATED INFORMATION OF NARROW-GAUGE RAILWAYS MENTIONED IN TEXT

| *Railway* | Gauge in | Length Miles | Opened Frt | Opened Pass | Reb'lt | Closed Frt | Closed Pass | Steam Locos | Act | Finance | Absorbed by |
|---|---|---|---|---|---|---|---|---|---|---|---|
| **PART I – BRITAIN** | | | | | | | | | | | |
| ASHOVER | 23½ | 7½ | 1924 | 1925 | | 1950 | 1936 | 5 | LRO | Private | |
| CAMPBELTOWN & MACHRIHANISH | 27 | 6 | 1877 | 1906 | 1906 | 1932 | 1932 | 4 | Pvte | Public | |
| CORRIS | 27 | 12¼ ① | 1859 | 1883 | 1883 | 1948 | 1931 | 4 | Pvte | Public | GWR 1931 |
| CROESOR | 23½ | 8 | 1864 | | | 1930 | 1936 | | Pvte | Public | WHR 1922 |
| EATON HALL | 15 | 3¾ | 1896 | | | 1946 | | 3 | | Private | |
| FAIRBOURNE | 24–15–12¼ | 2 | | 1890 | 1916 | | | 3 | | Private | |
| FESTINIOG | 23½ | 13½ | 1836 | 1863 | | 1946 | ② | 11 | Pvte | Public | |
| FESTINIOG & BLAENAU | 23½ | 3½ | 1868 | 1868 | 1883 | | 1960 | 2 | Pvte | Public | GWR 1883 |
| GLYN VALLEY | 28½ | 8¾ | 1873 | 1891 | 1891 | 1935 | 1933 | 4 | Pvte | Public | |
| GORSEDDAU | 23½ | 13 | 1875 | | | 1892 | | 1 | Pvte | Public | |
| HAFAN & TALYBONT | 27 | 7 | 1897 | 1897 | | 1898 | 1898 | 2 | Pvte | Public | |
| ISLE OF MAN incl Manx Northern | 36 | 46 | 1873–83 | 1873–83 | | 1971 | ③ | 16 | Pvte | Public | ③ |
| JERSEY | 54½–42 | 8½ | 1870 | 1870 | 1883 | 1936 | 1936 | 5 | Pvte | Public | |
| LEEK & MANIFOLD | 30 | 8½ | 1904 | 1904 | | 1934 | 1934 | 2 | LRO | Public | NSR 1904 |
| LLANDUDNO & COLWYN BAY | 42 | 8 | | 1907 | | | 1956 | | LRO | Public | |
| LYNTON & BARNSTAPLE | 23½ | 19½ | 1898 | 1898 | | 1935 | 1935 | 5 | Pvte | Public | SR 1923 |
| MANX ELECTRIC incl Snaefell | 36&42 | 23 | | 1893–99 | | | | | Pvte | Public | ④ |
| NANTLLE ⑤ | 42 | 9¼ | 1828 | 1850 | 1866pt | 1963 | 1866 | | Pvte | Public | LNWR 1866 |
| NORTH WALES NG | | 12¼ | 1877–81 | 1877–81 | | | 1916 | 5 | Pvte | Public | WHR 1922 |
| incl WHR | 23½ | 24 | | 1923 | | 1936 | 1936 | 3 | LRO | L/Auth | |
| PADARN | 23&48 | 7 | 1824 | | 1848 | 1965 | | 20 | Pvte | Private | |
| PENRHYN | 23 | 6 | 1801 | | 1876 | 1963 | | 30 | Pvte | Private | |
| RAVENGLASS & ESKDALE | 36–15 | 6¾ | 1875 | 1875 | ⑥ | ⑥ | | 2/5 | Pvte | Public | |
| ROMNEY HYTHE & DYMCHURCH | 15 | 13½ | 1927 | 1927 | | | | 11 | LRO | Private | |
| RYE & CAMBER | 36 | 2½ | | 1895 | | | 1939 | 2 | Pvte | Private | |
| SAND HUTTON | 15–18 | 7 | 1921 | 1912 | 1921 | 1932 | 1930 | 4 | LRO | Private | |
| SNOWDON MOUNTAIN | 31½ | 5 | | 1896 | 1897 | | | 7 | Pvte | Private | |
| SOUTHWOLD | 36 | 8½ | 1879 | 1879 | | 1929 | 1929 | 5 | Pvte | Private | |
| TALYLLYN | 27 | 7¼ | 1865 | 1865 | | 1952 | | 2/5 | Pvte | Private | |
| VALE OF RHEIDOL | 231/2 | 11¾ | 1902 | 1902 | | 1931 | ⑦ | 4 | LRO | Public | Camb. 1913; GWR 1922, BR 1948 VoR 1988 |
| Welsh Highland – see NWNG | | | | | | | | | | | |
| WELSHPOOL & LLANFAIR | 30 | 9 | 1903 | 1903 | | 1956 | 1931⑧ | 2/6 | LRO | Public | Camb. 1903; GWR 1922, BR 1948 |

*Notes:*

① Length reduced to 10 miles from c. 1867; steam and passenger working over 6¾ miles only

② Closed to passengers in 1939, reopened in stages 1954–1982

③ Whole system closed to all traffic 1966: Castletown–Port Erin section reopened, summer only, 1967: Douglas to Peel *and* Port Erin reopened, summer only, 1968: Douglas to Port Erin reopened on regular summer-only basis 1969. Taken over by Manx government 1 March 1972

④ Operation taken over by government agency 1958

⑤ Plateway with horse traction, part converted to standard gauge steam railway 1866

⑥ Original line closed to passengers 1908, to freight 1912. Rebuilt to 15in gauge by lease-holder and reopened in stages 1915–1917

⑦ Closed to normal traffic 1931 but seasonal service still operates. Sold to Brecon Mountain Railway 1988

⑧ Seven miles reopened for seasonal passenger traffic in stages by lessee, 1964–80

# TABULATED INFORMATION OF NARROW-GAUGE RAILWAYS
## MENTIONED IN TEXT (Continued)

| Railway | Gauge in | Length Miles | Opened Frt | Opened Pass | Reb'lt | Closed Frt | Closed Pass | Steam Locos | Act | Finance | Absorbed by |
|---|---|---|---|---|---|---|---|---|---|---|---|
| **PART II – IRELAND** | | | | | | | | | | | |
| BALLYCASTLE | 36 | 16 | 1880 | 1880 | | 1950 | 1950 | 5 | Pvte | BW Loan | NCC 1924 |
| BALLYMENA & LARNE | 36 | 31 | 1877–84 | 1877–84 | | 1942–50 | 1933 | 6 | Pvte | BW Loan | B&NC 1899 |
| BALLYMENA CUSHEN- DALL & RED BAY | 36 | 16½ | 1875–76 | 1886–88 | | 1936–40 | 1930 | 3 | Pvte | BW Loan | B&NC 1884 |
| BESSBROOK & NEWRY | 36 | 3 | 1885 | 1885 | | 1948 | 1948 | | Pvte | Public | |
| CASTLEDERG & VICTORIA BRIDGE | 36 | 7 | 1884 | 1884 | | 1933 | 1933 | 6 | Pvte | Part G'tee | |
| CAVAN & LEITRIM | 36 | 49 | 1887–8 | 1887–8 | | 1959 | 1959 | 9 | TA83 | G&L | GSR 1925 |
| CLOGHER VALLEY | 36 | 37 | 1887 | 1887 | | 1941 | 1941 | 7 | TA83 | G&L | |
| CORK, BLACKROCK & PASSAGE ⑨ | 63–36 | 16 | 1850 | 1850 | 1902–04 | 1932 | 1932 | 4 | Pvte | BW Loan | GSR 1925 |
| CORK & MUSKERRY | 36 | 26 | 1887–93 | 1887–93 | | 1934 | 1934 | 9 | TA83 | G&L | GSR 1925 |
| COUNTY DONEGAL *includes:* | | | | | | | | | | | |
| Finn Valley | 63–36 | 13 | 1863 | 1863 | 1894 | 1959 | 1959 | | Pvte | Public | DR 1892 |
| West Donegal | 36 | 18 | 1882–9 | 1882–9 | | 1959 | 1959 | | Pvte | G&L | DR 1892 |
| Donegal & K'begs | 36 | 19 | 1893 | 1893 | | 1959 | 1959 | see total below | RA89 | Grant | DR 1892 |
| Stranl'r & G'ties | 36 | 24 | 1895 | 1895 | | 1947 | 1947 | | RA89 | Grant | DR 1892 |
| Str'bne & Letterk'y | 36 | 19 | 1909 | 1909 | | 1959 | 1959 | | RA96 | G&L | ⑩ |
| Str'bne & Lond'dy | 36 | 14½ | 1900 | 1900 | | 1954 | 1954 | | RA96 | G&L | ⑪ |
| –Ballyshannon Br. | 36 | 15½ | 1905 | 1905 | | 1959 | 1959 | | RA96 | Grant | CDJR 1906 |
| Total of CDJC | | 123 | | | | | | 18 | | ⑫ | CDJR 1906 |
| GIANT'S CAUSEWAY PORTRUSH & BUSH VALLEY | 36 | 8 | 1883–7 | 1883–7 | | 1949 | 1949 | 4 | Pvte | BW Loan | |
| LISTOWEL & BALLYBUNION | ⑬ | 9 | 1888 | 1888 | | 1924 | 1924 | 3 | Pvte | Private | |
| LONDONDERRY & LOUGH SWILLY *includes:* | 63–36 | 14 | 1863 | 1863 | 1885 | 1953 | 1948 | | Pvte | Public | |
| Carndonagh | 36 | 18 | 1901 | 1901 | | 1935 | 1935 | see total below | RA96 | Grant | ⑭ |
| Letterkenny | 36 | 17 | 1883 | 1883 | | 1953 | 1948 | | Pvte | BW Loan | ⑭ |
| L'ky & Burtonp't | 36 | 50 | 1903 | 1903 | | 1947 | 1940 | | RA96 | Grant | ⑭ |
| Total of L&LR | | 99 | | | | | | 23 | | ⑫ | |
| SCHULL & SKIBBEREEN | 36 | 15 | 1886 | 1886 | | 1946 | 1946 | 6 | TA83 | G'tee | GSR 1925 |
| TRALEE & DINGLE | 36 | 37 | 1891 | 1891 | | 1947/53 | 1939 | 9 | TA83 | G'tee | GSR 1925 |
| WEST CLARE | 36 | 27 | 1887 | 1887 | | 1961 | 1961 | see table below | TA83 | G&L | GSR 1925 |
| *incl* South Clare | 36 | 26 | 1892 | 1892 | | 1961 | 1961 | | TA83 | G'tee | WCR 1892 |
| Total of WCR | | 53 | | | | | | 16 | | ⑫ | GSR 1925 |

*Notes (continued)*
⑨ Original 5ft 3in gauge line 6½ miles long; gauge converted 1902, extended 1904
⑩ Strabane & Letterkenny Rly remained independent till closure, but was worked by CDJR
⑪ Strabane & Londonderry Rly was owned by B&NCR/NCC but was worked by CDJR
⑫ Subsequent individual financial arrangements made with respective governments
⑬ Lartigue system monorail
⑭ Carndonagh, Letterkenny, and Burtonport Rlys remained independent until closure but were worked at all times by L&LSR

LRO – Light Railway Order    Pvte – Private Act of Parliament    TA83 – Tramways Act 1883
RA89 – Railways Act 1889    RA96 – Railways Act 1896
Private – Capital subscribed privately    Public – Capital subscribed by public
Grant – Railway built wholly or mainly with government grant
BW Loan – Railway built largely with money lent by Board of Works, remainder subscribed by public
L/Auth – Railway built largely with money found by local authorities, remainder by public
G'tee – Whole share capital, nil loan capital guaranteed by state and local authorities
Part G'tee – 75 per cent only of share capital and no loans guaranteed by local authority
G&L – Both share and loan capital wholly guaranteed by state and local authorities jointly

# BIBLIOGRAPHY

Boyd, J.I.C. *Narrow Gauge Rails to Portmadoc* (Oakwood Press 1949)
*Narrow Gauge Rails in Mid Wales* (Oakwood Press 1952)
*Festiniog Railway Vols I & II* (Oakwood Press 1960)
*Isle of Man Railway* (Oakwood Press 1962)
*Narrow Gauge Rails in South Caernarvonshire* (Oakwood Press 1972)
*Narrow Gauge Rails in North Caernarvonshire* Vol 1 (West)
    (Oakwood Press 1981)
Brown, Prideaux & Radcliffe *Lynton & Barnstaple Railway*
    (David & Charles 1971)
Catchpole, L.T. *The Lynton & Barnstaple Railway*
    (Oakwood Press 1936)
Davies, D.L. *The Glyn Valley Tramway* (Oakwood Press 1962)
Davies, W.J.K. *The Vale of Rheidol Railway* (Ian Allan Ltd 1961)
Fayle, H. *Narrow Gauge Railways of Ireland*
    (Greenlake Publications 1946)
Kichenside, G.M. *Source Book of Miniature & Narrow Gauge Railways*
    (Ward Lock 1981)
Macnab, I. *History of the Isle of Man Railway* (Greenlake
    Publications 1943)
'Manifold' *The Leek & Manifold Valley Railway* (J.H. Henstock 1955)
Patterson, E.M. *The County Donegal Railways* (David & Charles 1962)
*The Londonderry & Lough Swilly Railway* (David & Charles 1964)
*The Ballycastle Railway* (David & Charles 1965)
*The Ballymena Lines* (David & Charles 1968)
Prideaux, J.D.C.A. *The Welsh Narrow Gauge Railway*
    (David & Charles 1976)
*The English Narrow Gauge Railway* (David & Charles 1978)
*The Irish Narrow Gauge Railway* (David & Charles 1981)
Rolt, L.T.C. & Whitehouse, P.B. *Lines of Character* (Constable 1952)
Spooner, C.E. *Narrow Gauge Railways*
Stephenson Locomotive Society, the *Journal* of
Whitehouse, P.B. *Festiniog Railway Revival* (Ian Allan 1963)
    *On the Narrow Gauge* (Thomas Nelson 1963)
Whitehouse, P.B. & Powell, J. *The Tralee & Dingle Railway*
    (Locomotive Publishing Co 1958)

# INDEX